THE
BOOK OF
WISDOM
AND
WIT

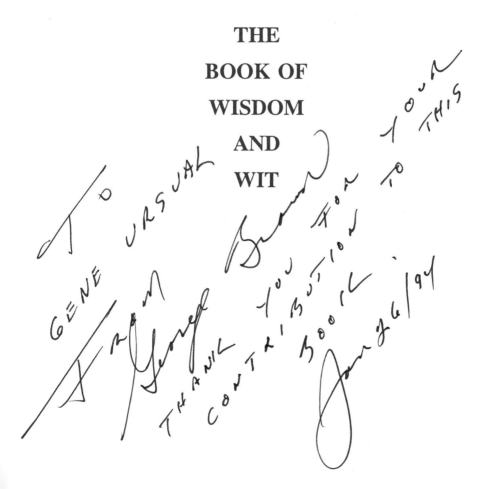

To

GENE URSUAL

From

George Brown

THANK YOU FOR YOUR
CONTRIBUTION TO THIS
BOOK

Jan 26/94

By the Same Author

THE FENIAN RAIDS 1866-70
THE NORTHWEST REBELLION 1885
CONSPICUOUS GALLANTRY MEDAL
THOSE WHO DARED
CANADIAN WING COMMANDERS
CANADIAN WELCOME HOME MEDALS
COMMANDO GALLANTRY AWARDS
LLOYDS WAR MEDALS FOR BRAVERY AT SEA
FOR DISTINGUISHED CONDUCT IN THE FIELD

THE
BOOK OF
WISDOM
AND
WIT

1,000 QUOTATIONS

MANY OF THE WORLDS MOST FAMOUS

PLUS

OVER 700 PROVERBS

Written and compiled by

GEORGE A. BROWN

Western Canadian Distributors Ltd.

Brown, George A.
The Book of Wisdom and Wit/George A. Brown
ISBN 0-9695136-1-5: $12.95

Published 1994 by

Western Canadian Distributors Ltd.,
P. O. Box 3095,
Langley, B. C., V3A 4R3,
Canada.

Dedicated to my family

Editorial Note

This book does not have an index as it is not intended to be used as a reference but instead as a book that can be picked up and set down at any time. One that could be referred to throughout one's life. A book that may induce inspiration and humour whenever required. An opportunity to fill a small space in time when available, as there should always be time to think about thinking.

George A. Brown

ACKNOWLEDGEMENT

To Marion Fraser

Who has been my right arm for twenty years.

Who, regardless of how much work there was

to do, has always been ready, willing and

able to do more; and who, if my inspiration ever

waned, was always capable of picking up the

speed. A lady for whom the impossible does not exist

and who blends Saturday and Sunday into the work week

like any other day and likewise is capable of producing

miracles. She has the power to stimulate everyone

around her with her competent and positive attitude.

Her loyal commitment, dedication and friendship

I cherish.

Marion - Thank you.

ACKNOWLEDGEMENTS

I am indebted and grateful to all those that have assisted in so many ways in bringing this book to completion.

Eleanor Alexander, Sonya Axelson, Chuck Bainbridge, Gary Bates, George Batey, Dorothy Baye, David Blair, Jack Boddington, Joan Boddington, Greg Brown, John Brown, Lori Ann Brown, Margo Brown, Margot Brown, Joy Bruce, Rob Bruce, Darlene Cameron, Larry Davis, Kendall DeMenech, Wendy Fraser, Charmaine Goudreau, Bernie Grinstead, Don Hall, Gale Hawkes, Joy Hawkes, Al Jensen, Robbie Johnson, Vicky Kidd, Kim Kilborn, Hugh King, Pamela King, Bernhard Lachkovics, Cheryl Lachkovics, Esther McFarlane, Paul McFarlane, Stewart McIntosh, Craig MacAllister, Gladys MacAllister, Len Matthews, Irene Maule, Brian Parkinson, Lorna Penhall, Ron Penhall, Kirk Poje, Marie Posivak, Gary Putnam, Maurice Raphael, Brenda Rorvik, Mia Schokker, Betty Schopff, Dawn Skarratt, Mick Skarratt, Jeannie Sluggett, Tanya Strand, Syndi Stuart, John Tamplin, Alisen Thibault, Robert Thompson, Merv Thurgood, Geoff Todd, Eugene Ursual, Anne Werry, Helen Werry, Ray Willie, Dennis Wood, Wendy Wood.

FRONT COVER DESIGN
"ARTIST"
Arnie Fisk

PHOTOGRAPHY - BACK COVER
INFINITY PHOTOGRAPHICS
John and Janice Woods
Fort Langley, B. C.

CAREERS INCORPORATED LTD.
Linda and Glen Thibault
Clearbrook, B. C.

MICROAGE "THE SOLUTION STORE"
Ian Brett
Langley, B. C.

HIGNELL PRINTING
Geoff Todd
488 Burnell Street
Winnipeg, Manitoba

FORWARD

Readers, writers, comedians and public speakers have long found quotation references to be a great source of inspiration and a significant tool for reinforcing and enhancing ones expressions.

Everyone, at sometime, has found himself groping for a word or words to describe the idea he wishes to convey. The words of others aptly employed move us to a new understanding and shared realization about our world and life experiences.

It is not uncommon for speechmakers, journalists and reporters to consult quotation collections frequently to further the impact of their writings. Some authors have achieved status and fame through their unforgettable quotations. Many of these quotations have been profound and together some have even achieved immortality. Quotations are the net result or the summation of a paragraph, a whole page or maybe even the story. The ability to choose the right word in the right place at the right time.

Mark Twain once wrote:

"A powerful agent is the right word, whenever we come upon one of those intensely right words - the resulting effect is physical as well as spiritual and electrically prompt."

Aldous Huxley wrote:

"Words form the thread on which we string our experiences."

Confucius wrote:

"Without knowing the force of words, it is impossible to know men."

Kipling wrote:

"Words are, of course, the most powerful drug used by mankind".

Edward Thorndike wrote:

"Colours fade, temples crumble, empires fall, but wise words endure".

There is no doubt that when we talk about wisdom we perceive wisdom to be success and success is to many people different things. It can mean power, money, happiness, freedom, recognition, security, victory, triumph, affluence or prosperity.

One of the best descriptions that I have ever read, with respect to success, came from Bessie Anderson Stanley from Lincoln, Kansas in 1904. She wrote:

"He has achieved success who has lived well, laughed often and loved much; who has enjoyed the trust of pure women, the respect of intelligent men and the love of little children; who has filled his niche, and accomplished his task; who has left the world better than he found it, whether by an improved poppy, a perfect poem, or a rescued soul; who has never lacked appreciation of earth's beauty, or failed to express it; who has always looked for the best in others and given them the best he had; whose life was an inspiration; whose memory a benediction."

Rudyard Kipling wrote one of the most famous poems of all time with respect to success:

IF

If you can keep your head when all about you are losing theirs and blaming it on you;

If you can trust yourself when all men doubt you, but make allowance for their doubting too:

If you can wait and not be tired by waiting, or, being lied about, don't deal in lies, or being hated don't give way to hating, and yet don't look too good, nor talk too wise;

If you can dream -- and not make dreams your master;

If you can think -- and not make thoughts your aim,

If you can meet with Triumph and Disaster and treat those two impostors just the same;

If you can bear to hear the truth you've spoken twisted by knaves to make a trap for fools, or watch the things you gave your life to, broken and stoop and build 'em up with worn-out tools;

If you can make one heap of all your winnings and risk it on one turn of pitch-and-toss, and lose, and start again at your beginnings, and never breathe a word about your loss:

If you can force your heart and nerve and sinew to serve your turn long after they are gone, and so hold on when there is nothing in you except the Will which says to them: "Hold on!"

If you can talk with crowds and keep your virtue, or walk with Kings -- nor lose the common touch,

If neither foes nor loving friends can hurt you,

If all men count with you, but none too much:

If you can fill the unforgiving minute with sixty seconds' worth of distance run, Yours is the Earth and everything that's in it.

And -- which is more -- you'll be a Man, my son!

Rudyard Kipling

*"**T**he two most engaging powers of an author are to make new things familiar and familiar things new".*

William Makepeace Thackeray

This book presents a compelling mix of timeless wisdom, wit and intelligence on matters of both far reaching and immediate significance.

George A. Brown

"**I**f a man empties his purse into his head, no man can take it away from him. An investment in knowledge always pays the best interest".

Benjamin Franklin

*"**A** man's legs must be long enough to reach the ground".*

Abraham Lincoln

Courage and determination are the two most important ingredients to success.

George A. Brown

Every great commanding moment in the annals of the world is the triumph of some enthusiasm.

Ralph Waldo Emerson

Give me a lever long enough and a prop strong enough, I can single handedly move the world.

Archimedes

I expect to pass through life but once. If, therefore, there be any kindness I can show, or any good thing I can do to any fellow being, let me do it now, for I shall not pass this way again.

William Penn

Smile ... its the second best thing you can do with your lips.

It's a funny thing about life, if you refuse to accept anything but the best, you very often get it.

W. Somerset Maugham

No one can make you feel inferior without your consent.

Eleanor Roosevelt

Treasure the love you receive above all. It will survive long after your gold and good health have vanished.

Og Mandino

We trained hard...but it seemed that every time we were beginning to form up into teams we would be reorganized. I was to learn later in life that we tend to meet any new situation by reorganizing: and a wonderful method it can be for creating the illusion of progress while producing confusion, inefficiency and demoralization.

Petronious Arbiter 210 B.C.

If at first you don't succeed...well so much for sky diving.

There are many things that we would throw away, if we were not afraid that others might pick them up.

Oscar Wilde

Some men see things as they are and say why - I see things that never were and say why not.

George Bernard Shaw

A wise man will make more opportunities than he finds.

Francis Bacon

Let the refining and improving of your own life keep you so busy that you have little time to criticize others.

Unknown

There's no fool like an old fool - you can't beat experience!

The desire of knowledge, like the thirst of riches, increases ever with the acquisition of it.

Laurence Sterne

No problem can stand the assault of sustained thinking.

Voltaire

We know too much and feel too little. At least we feel too little of those creative emotions from which a good life springs.

Bertrand Russell

Many receive advice, only the wise profit from it.

Publilius Syrus

If you could only kick the person who is most responsible for most of your troubles, you wouldn't be able to sit down.

It doesn't take a hero to order men into battle. It takes a hero to be one of those men who goes into battle.

General H. Normann Schwarzkopf

Discussion is an exchange of knowledge; argument an exchange of ignorance.

Robert Quillen

Experience is not what happens to a man, it is what a man does with what happens to him.

Aldous Huxley

If you betray someone's confidentiality you stand to lose their confidence forever.

George A. Brown

Lady to handsome man: "You look like my third husband".
Him: "How many have you had?"
Lady: "Just two."

I'm opposed to millionaires, but it would be dangerous to offer me the position.

Mark Twain

I'd like to be rich enough so I could throw soap away after the letters are worn off.

Andy Rooney

Happiness depends upon ourselves.

Aristotle

Nine-tenths of wisdom is being wise in time.

Theodore Roosevelt

A man claims his wife lost her credit cards but he hasn't reported it because whoever stole them spends less than she did.

Men stumble over the truth from time to time, but most pick themselves up and hurry off as if nothing happened.

Winston S. Churchill

Democracy gives two fools twice the power of a wise man.

Unknown

Mankind must put an end to war or war will put an end to mankind.

John F. Kennedy

The poorest of all men is not the one without a cent.
It's the man without a dream.

Unknown

They say hard work never killed anyone, but why take a chance on being the first casualty.

When the going gets tough, the tough get going.

Unknown

Show me a good loser and I will show you a loser.

Paul Newman

There is no victory without pursuit.

Napoleon I

Don't judge me by my medals ..... judge me by my scars.

Merv F. Thurgood

A lot of good arguments are spoiled by some guy who knows what he's talking about.

Determination is the wake up call to human will.

Anthony Robbins

To apologize sincerely as an adult is a lesson learned well as a child.

George A. Brown

When I was a kid my parents moved a lot - but I always found them.

Rodney Dangerfield

Progress always involves risk; you can't steal second base and keep your foot on first.

Frederick Wilcox

I don't care what the world knows about me, I just hope my mother never finds out.

I don't know the key to success, but the key to failure is trying to please everybody.

Bill Cosby

That this nation, under God, shall have a new birth of freedom, and that government of the people, by the people, and for the people, shall not perish from the earth.

Abraham Lincoln

Democracy is the form of government in which the free are rulers.

Aristotle

There is no knowledge that is not power.

Ralph Waldo Emerson

A fool and his money are better than no date at all.

Sweet flowers are slow and weeds make haste.

William Shakespeare

To be conscious that you are ignorant is a great step to knowledge.

Benjamin Disraeli

One thing is certain today - the illiterates are definitely not the least intelligent among us.

Henry Miller

Bad excuses are worse than none.

Thomas Fuller

Be like a duck - above the surface look composed and unruffled - below the surface, paddle like crazy.

Familiarity breeds contempt - and children.

Mark Twain

Success is a journey, not a destination.

Ben Sweetland

You can inherit wealth, but never wisdom.

Unknown

Chance favours the prepared mind.

Louis Pasteur

Telling your teenagers the facts of life is like giving a fish a bath!

The only good is knowledge and the only evil is ignorance.

Socrates

Every great achievement was once considered impossible.

Unknown

When an archer misses the mark, he turns and looks for the fault within himself. Failure to hit the bulls-eye is never the fault of the target. To improve your aim, improve yourself.

Gilbert Arland

No one has ever been rewarded for the things he intended to do.

George A. Brown

Poverty: a state of mind brought on by a neighbour's new car.

When desire dies, fear is born.

Baltasar Gracian

October. This is one of the peculiarly dangerous months to speculate in stocks.
The others are July, January, September, April, November, May, March, June,
December, August, and February.

Mark Twain

Choose a job you love, and you will never have to work a day in your life.

Confucius

Habit is either the best of servants or the worst of masters.

Nathaniel Emmons

Sex is the most fun I ever had without laughing.

Woody Allen

We shall be judged more by what we do at home than what we preach abroad.

John F. Kennedy

I am only one; but still I am one. I cannot do everything, but still I can do something; I will not refuse to do the something I can do.

Helen Keller

You cannot create experience. You must undergo it.

Albert Camus

Ability is of little account without opportunity.

Napoleon 1

One of life's greatest disappointments is finding that the guy who writes the ads for the bank is not the same guy who makes the loans.

Work without purpose is like shovelling smoke.

Jack Boddington

To do what we have to learn, we learn by doing.

Aristotle

Courage is resistance to fear, mastery of fear, not absence of fear.

Mark Twain

The next best thing to knowing something is knowing where to find it.

Samuel Johnson

It costs no more to go first class - you just can't stay as long.

Hold yourself responsible for a higher standard than anyone else expects of you. Never excuse yourself.

Henry Ward Beecher

There are two levers for moving men - interest and fear.

Napoleon I

In matters of style, swim with the current; in matters of principle, stand like a rock.

Thomas Jefferson

Be generous with praise and cautious with promises.

George A. Brown

People always seem to drive better when I'm not in a rush.

As soon as you cannot keep anything from a woman, you love her.

Paul Geraldy

To be prepared for war is one of the most effectual means of preserving peace.

George Washington

We first make our habits and then our habits make us.

John Dryden

He has achieved success who has lived well, laughed often, and loved much.

Bessie Anderson Stanley

Budget: a mathematical confirmation of your suspicions.

Uneasy lies the head that wears a crown.

William Shakespeare

Men are wise in proportion not to their experiences, but to their capacity for experience.

Unknown

There is only one thing in the world worse than being talked about, and that is not being talked about.

Oscar Wilde

If you want a thing done well, do it yourself.

Napoleon I

Always yield to temptation....it might not pass your way again.

One man with courage is a majority.

Andrew Jackson

The display of status symbols is usually a result of low self-esteem. The self-confident person can afford to project a modest image.

Unknown

Action is the antidote to desire.

Joan Baez

I have nothing to offer but blood, toil, tears and sweat.

Winston S. Churchill

A child is a person who can't understand why someone would give away a perfectly good cat.

There is no future in any job. The future lies in the man who holds the job.

George Crane

Enthusiasm and success go together.

George A. Brown

No objects of value...are worth risking the priceless experience of waking up one more day.

Jack Smith

By all means marry; if you get a good wife, you'll become happy; if you get a bad one, you'll become a philosopher.

Socrates

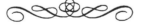

The person who coined "Out of sight...Out of mind" had no children of dating age out on Saturday night.

When I was a boy of fourteen, my father was so ignorant I could hardly stand to have the old man around. But when I got to be twenty-one, I was astonished at how much he had learned in seven years.

Mark Twain

An army marches on its stomach.

Napoleon I

When I warned the French that Britain would fight on alone whatever they did, their generals told their prime minister and his divided cabinet "In three weeks England will have her neck wrung like a chicken" - some chicken, some neck.

Winston S. Churchill

Love doesn't sit there like a stone, it has to be made, like bread; remade all the time, made new.

Ursula K. Le Guin

By the time a man realizes that maybe his father was right, he usually has a son that thinks he's wrong.

Charles Wadsworth

Real generosity is doing something nice for someone who'll never find it out.

Frank A. Clark

There is perhaps nothing so bad and so dangerous in life as fear.

Jawaharlal Nehru

An autobiography usually reveals nothing bad about its writer except his memory.

Franklin P. Jones

A friend is a gift you give yourself.

Robert Louis Stevenson

A diamond is a chunk of coal that made good under pressure!

Honesty is the first chapter in the book of wisdom.

Thomas Jefferson

To be without some of the things you want is an indispensable part of happiness.

Bertrand Russell

The nation had the lion's heart. I had the luck to give the roar.

Winston S. Churchill

Success is getting what you want. Happiness is liking what you get.

Unknown

Marriages are made in heaven...so are thunder and lightning.

Most people are about as happy as they make up their minds to be.

Abraham Lincoln

Now this is not the end. It is not even the beginning of the end, but is perhaps, the end of the beginning.

Winston S. Churchill

I have never been bored in the presence of a happy person.

George A. Brown

The quality of a person's life is in direct proportion to their commitment to excellence, regardless of their chosen field of endeavor.

Vince Lombardi

One way to save face is to keep the lower half shut.

Conversation means being able to disagree and still continue the conversation.

Dwight MacDonald

You are the same today that you'll be five years from now except for two things: the people you meet and the books you read.

Mac McMillan

It is very hard to be simple enough to be good.

Ralph Waldo Emerson

People ask you for criticism, but they only want praise.

W. Somerset Maugham

I gave up smoking, drinking and sex - it was the worst hour of my life!

Man's mind stretched to a new idea never goes back to its original dimensions.

Oliver Wendell Holmes

Learning is a matter of attitude, not aptitude.

Georgi Lozanov

Why shouldn't truth be stranger than fiction? Fiction, after all, has to make sense.

Mark Twain

Personally, I'm always ready to learn, although I do not always like being taught.

Winston S.Churchill

To get maximum attention, it's hard to beat a good, big mistake!

In war, resolution; in defeat, defiance; in victory, magnanimity; in peace, goodwill.

Winston S. Churchill

The buck stops here.

Harry S. Truman

It is always a good idea to speak the truth, unless, of course, you are a good liar.

Jerome K. Jerome

If you desire many things, many things will seem but a few.

Benjamin Franklin

Don't you wish that all those people trying to find themselves would just get lost!

We lift ourselves by our thoughts, we climb upon our vision ourselves.

Orison Swett Marden

Women are never disarmed by compliments. Men always are.

Oscar Wilde

Whatever you don't receive at home you will balance the scale somewhere else.

George A. Brown

If you have never been hated by your child, you have never been a parent.

Bette Davis

My husband's idea of a seven-course dinner is a roll of bologna and a six-pack.

I must govern the clock, not be governed by it.

Golda Meir

No opportunity is ever lost; someone else picks those you miss.

Unknown

I did not have three thousand pairs of shoes, I had one thousand and sixty.

Imelda Marcos

Slow and steady wins the race.

Aesop

I'm making my favourite thing for dinner - Reservations!

I'm extraordinarily patient provided I get my own way in the end.

Margaret Thatcher

No country, company or household has ever been able to borrow, spend or tax itself into prosperity...so, why does our government try?

Merv F. Thurgood

It's easier to obtain forgiveness than to obtain permission.

David H. Blair

There are defeats more triumphant than victories.

Michel de Montaigne

She's a light eater - As soon as it's light she starts eating!

Imagination is more important than knowledge.

Albert Einstein

Boldness, without the rules of propriety, becomes insubordination.

Confucius

How many good books suffer neglect through the inefficiency of their beginnings!

Edgar Allan Poe

Confidence is contagious. So is the lack of confidence.

Michael O'Brien

There are three types of people: Those who make it happen; those who watch it happen; and those who sit around and say - "What the heck's happening?"

You must either conquer and rule or serve and lose, suffer or triumph, be the anvil or the hammer.

Johann Wolfgang Von Goethe

Laugh and the world laughs with you; snore and you sleep alone.

Anthony Burgess

A throne is only a bench covered with velvet.

Napoleon I

More amenities does not mean more happiness. More happiness does not mean more amenities.

George A. Brown

Why is the one person who snores always the first one to fall asleep?

The way I see it, if you want the rainbow, you gotta put up with the rain.

Dolly Parton

There is nothing either good or bad but thinking makes it so.

William Shakespeare

Nothing great will ever be achieved without great men, and men are great only if they are determined to be so.

Charles Degaulle

The passion to get ahead is sometimes born of the fear lest we be left behind.

Eric Hoffer

I like to do all the talking myself. It saves time and prevents arguments.

You will find as you look back upon your life that the moments when you have really lived are the moments when you have done things in the spirit of love.

Henry Drummond

Happiness is not an absence of problems; but the ability to deal with them.

Unknown

If we encounter a man of rare intellect, we should ask him what books he reads.

Ralph Waldo Emerson

The bitter and the sweet come from the outside, the hard from within, from one's own efforts.

Albert Einstein

Why do banks say we should trust them when they turn around and chain down the pens.

Well done is better than well said.

Benjamin Franklin

Happiness is not a state to arrive at, but a manner of travelling.

Margaret Lee Runbeck

It is better to wear out than to rust out.

Bishop Richard Cumberland

I quote others only the better to express myself.

Michel de Montaigne

It's easy to identify people who can't count to 10. They're in front of you in the market express lane.

If you're looking for a big opportunity, seek out a big problem.

Unknown

Never have a $1,000 meeting to solve a $100 problem.

George A. Brown

If sex is such a natural phenomenon, how come there are so many books on how to?

Bette Midler

When I was young there was no respect for the young, and now that I am old there is no respect for the old. I missed out coming and going.

J. B. Priestly

Never go to bed mad. Stay up and fight.

Phyllis Diller

There is no experience better for the heart than reaching down and lifting people up.

John Andrew Holmer

Don't get mad, get even.

Joseph P. Kennedy

When written in Chinese, the word **crisis** is composed of two characters one represents danger and the other represents opportunity.

John F. Kennedy

I would rather be a beggar and single than a queen and married.

Queen Elizabeth I

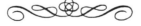

If the fur is on the outside and the skin is on the inside..then the outside is the furside and the inside is the skinside.

If you pick up a starving dog and make him prosperous, he will not bite you. This is the principal difference between a dog and a man.

Mark Twain

Geography has made us (U. S. A. and Canada) neighbours. History has made us friends. Economics has made us partners. And necessity has made us allies. Those whom nature hath so joined together, let no man put asunder.

John F. Kennedy

Genius is one percent inspiration and ninety-nine percent perspiration.

Thomas Edison

Fools rush in where angels fear to tread.

Alexander Pope

Never play leapfrog with a unicorn.

In the confrontation between the stream and the rock, the stream always wins - not through strength but by perseverance.

Unknown

We can destroy ourselves by cynicism and disillusion just as effectively as by bombs.

Kenneth Clark

I never think of the future. It comes soon enough.

Albert Einstein

You can accomplish by kindness what you cannot by force.

Publilius Syrus

Middle age is that time of life when you can feel bad in the morning without having had fun the night before.

In response to Lord Sandwich's opinion that John Wilkes would die "either of the pox or on the gallows" - "that will depend on whether I embrace Your Lordship's mistress or Your Lordship's principles".

John Wilkes

Keep your face to the sunshine and you cannot see the shadow.

Helen Keller

It takes a lot of effort to become the person that you wished you were.

George A. Brown

Oh, it is excellent to have a giant's strength, but it is tyrannous to use it like a giant.

Unknown

The stork is too often held responsible for circumstances that might better be attributed to a lark.

Golf is a game whose aim is to hit a very small ball into an even smaller hole, with weapons singularly ill-designed for the purpose.

Winston S. Churchill

Nobody talks more of free enterprise and competition and of the best man winning than the man who inherited his father's store or farm.

C. Wright Mills

Thorough preparation must lead to success. Neglect nothing.

Lt/Gen Sir Arthur Currie

One friend in a lifetime is much; two are many; three are hardly possible.

Henry Brooks Adams

No man was ever shot while doing the dishes.

Success seems to be largely a matter of hanging on after others have let go.

William Feather

I disapprove of what you say, but I will defend to the death your right to say it.

Voltaire

The people who say, "Money isn't everything," usually have plenty of it.

Unknown

Problems are opportunities in work clothes.

Henry Kaiser

The man who says that marriage is a 50-50 proposition doesn't understand two things....1. Women, 2. Fractions.

Men always want to be a woman's first love; women have a more subtle instinct: what they like is to be a man's last romance.

Unknown

We don't know one millionth of one percent about anything.

Thomas Edison

A people which is able to say everything becomes able to do everything.

Napoleon I

Freedom's just another word for nothing left to lose.

Kris Kristofferson

If women are so smart, why do they always dance backwards?

It is better to die on your feet than to live on your knees.

Dolores Ibarruri

To get the right answer, you have to ask the right question.

Unknown

We turn not older with years, but newer every day.

Emily Dickinson

Good health is true wealth.

George A. Brown

All men are not homeless, but some are home less than others.

Happiness is having a large, loving, caring, close-knit family in another city.

George Burns

Speak well of your enemies - remember, you made them!

Unknown

There are three kinds of lies - lies, damned lies and statistics.

Mark Twain

A promise made is a debt unpaid.

Robert Service

The average girl would rather have beauty than brains, because the average man can see better than he can think.

Never let a day go by without giving at least three people a compliment.

Unknown

Laughter has no foreign accent.

Paul Lowney

Certainly a leader needs a clear vision of the organization and where it is going, but a vision is of little value unless it is shared in a way so as to generate enthusiasm and commitment. Leadership and communication are inseparable.

Claude I. Taylor

When angry, count four; when very angry, swear.

Mark Twain

Golf is like sex: When it's good, it's terrific, and when it's bad, it's still pretty good.

Flying is hours of sheer boredom interrupted by moments of stark terror.

Unknown

A fool always finds a greater fool to admire him.

Nicolas Boileau

There is but one step from the sublime to the ridiculous.

Napoleon I

The maxim of the British people is "Business as usual."

Winston S. Churchill

Some men need two women in their life. A secretary to take things down, and a wife to pick things up.

Who is more foolish, the child afraid of the dark or the man afraid of the light?

Maurice Freehill

Each man has a choice in life: he may approach it as a creator or critic, a lover or a hater, a giver or a taker.

Unknown

We are all accountable for our actions, even if we don't think we are.

George A. Brown

There are two times in a man's life when he should not speculate: when he can't afford it, and when he can.

Mark Twain

If you wait too long to marry your dreamboat, you may find, by the time you have made up your mind, his cargo has shifted.

I would prefer even to fail with honour than win by cheating.

Sophocles

What is a cynic? A man who knows the price of everything, and the value of nothing.

Oscar Wilde

Half of the results of a good intention are evil; half the results of an evil intention are good.

Mark Twain

The people who get on in this world are the people who get up and look for the circumstances they want, and, if they can't find them, make them.

George Bernard Shaw

An allowance is what you pay your children to live with you.

The most creative ideas come from beginners - not from experts.

Unknown

Even if you're going down the right road, keep up the pace or someone will pass you.

George A. Brown

A bore is a fellow talker who can change the subject to his topic of conversation faster than you can change it back to yours.

Laurence J. Peter

You can't build a reputation on what you are **going** to do.

Henry Ford

An optimist is a fellow who believes a housefly is looking for a way to get out.

George Jean Nathan

The one means that wins the easiest victory over reason: terror and force.

Adolf Hitler

An idea isn't responsible for the people who believe in it.

Don Morquis

Kindness in words creates confidence. Kindness in thinking creates profoundness. Kindness in giving creates love.

Lao-tzu

We don't receive wisdom; we must discover it for ourselves after a journey that no one can take for us or spare us.

Marcel Proust

I always wanted to be somebody but I should have been more specific.

Lily Tomlin

Regardless of how little you have, you can always give encouragement.

Unknown

It's not hard to make decisions when you know what your values are.

Roy Disney

The pen is mightier that the sword.

Bulwer-Lytton

Our lives begin to end the day we become silent about things that matter.

Martin Luther King, Jr.

When a man brings home flowers for no reason, there's a reason.

It is much easier to be critical than correct.

Benjamin Disraeli

Be nice to people on your way up because you'll meet'em on your way down.

Wilson Mizner

Rules are to be used with intelligence and latitudes - therefore the guidance of wisemen and the compliance of fools.

Unknown

Power corrupts the few, while weakness corrupts the many.

Eric Hoffer

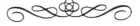

There is one advantage in being married. You can't make a fool of yourself without knowing it.

I lived in solitude in the country and noticed how the monotony of a quiet life stimulates the creative mind.

Albert Einstein

Too bad all the people who know how to run the country are busy driving cabs and cutting hair.

George Burns

Talk low, talk slow, and don't say too much.

John Wayne

Age is only important with Scotch and Cheese.

George A. Brown

If at first you don't succeed, try, try, again. Then quit. There's no use being a damn fool about it.

W. C. Fields

It is not best to swap horses while crossing the river.

Abraham Lincoln

The violence we do to ourselves in order to remain faithful to the one we love is hardly better than an act of infidelity.

Francois de la Rochefoucauld

When grace is joined with wrinkles, it is adorable. There is an unspeakable dawn in happy old age.

Victor Hugo

Time flies, and what is past is done.

Johann Wolfgang Von Goethe

Every year it takes less time to fly across the ocean, and longer to drive to work.

Doing easily what others find difficult is talent; doing what is impossible for talent is genius.

Henri Frederic Amiel

Oh, the difference between nearly right and exactly right.

Unknown

Remember always that you have not only the right to be an individual, you have an obligation to be one.

Eleanor Roosevelt

Some of us treat our bodies as if we had a spare in the trunk.

Unknown

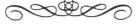

Doctors will tell you that if you eat slowly, you will eat less. That is particularly true if you are a member of a large family.

Two wrongs don't make a right, but they make a good excuse.

Thomas Szasz

Use it or lose it.

Jimmy Connors

Whether women are better than men I cannot say - but I can say they are certainly no worse.

Golda Meir

All the knowledge I possess everyone else can acquire, but my heart is all my own.

Johann Wolfgang Von Goethe

Those in the cheaper seats clap. The rest of you rattle your jewellery.

John Lennon

A mystic bond of brotherhood makes all men one.

Thomas Carlyle

It is an unfortunate fact that we can secure peace only by preparing for war.

John F. Kennedy

Silence is the most perfect expression of scorn.

George Bernard Shaw

Anger manages everything poorly.

George A. Brown

Sign in a bankrupt store window - "We undersold everyone".

The wheel that squeaks the loudest is the one that gets the grease.

Josh Billings

No man is an island, entire of itself; every man is a piece of the continent.

John Donne

Tomorrow doesn't matter, for I have lived today.

Horace

Of cheerfulness, or a good temper - the more it is spent, the more it remains.

Ralph Waldo Emerson

Time may be a great healer, but it's a lousy beautician.

The final forming of a person's character lies in their own hands.

Anne Frank

The books that the world calls immoral are the books that show the world its own shame.

Oscar Wilde

He'd be sharper than a serpent's tooth, if he wasn't as dull as ditch water.

Charles Dickens

Audacity augments courage; hesitation, fear.

Publilius Syrus

Standing in the middle of the road is very dangerous; you get knocked down by the traffic from both sides.
Margaret Thatcher

Believe only half of what you see and nothing that you hear.

Dinah Mulock Craik

Put not your trust in money, but put your money in trust.

Oliver Wendell Holmes, Sr.

The only thing worse than being old and bent is being young and broke.

Unknown

Start not with a word, but with a deed.

Florence Nightingale

It goes without saying that you should never have more children that you have car windows.

Erma Bombeck

If you take good care of your employees, they will take good care of your customers.

George A. Brown

The reason talk is cheap is that the supply always exceeds the demand.

Unknown

If you were to sell your character, would you get full retail, or would it go for a bargain-basement price?

Unknown

A man without scars has never battled for his beliefs.

E.G. Ursual

No matter how much cats fight, there always seem to be plenty of kittens.

Abraham Lincoln

You can do anything in this world if you are prepared to take the consequences.

W. Somerset Maugham

How much better is it to weep at joy than to joy at weeping!

William Shakespeare

There is more power in the open hand than in the clenched fist.

Herbert N. Casson

To go beyond is as wrong as to fall short.

Confucius

Give a boy enough rope and he'll bring home a stray dog on the end of it.

Everything happens to everybody sooner or later if there is time enough.

George Bernard Shaw

Never give a sucker an even break.

W.C. Fields

The paths of glory lead but to the grave.

Thomas Gray

It is better to be looked over than overlooked.

Mae West

Misers aren't fun to live with, but they make wonderful ancestors.

David Brenner

An object in possession seldom retains the same charm that it had in pursuit.

Pliny the Younger

Look at me: I worked my way up from nothing to a state of extreme poverty.

Groucho Marx

I think and think for months and years. Ninety-nine times, the conclusion is false. The hundredth time I am right.

Albert Einstein

One can never consent to creep when one feels an impulse to soar.

Helen Keller

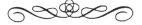

I do not believe in an afterlife, although I am bringing a change of underwear.

Woody Allen

Three may keep a secret if two of them are dead.

Benjamin Franklin

The basic character of a man has been formed by the time he is six.

George A. Brown

All the things I really like to do are either immoral, illegal, or fattening.

Alexander Woollcott

Forgive me my nonsense as I also forgive the nonsense of those who think they can talk sense.

Robert Frost

Before you accuse your husband of infidelity...pause to reflect. He may have been faithful to you dozens of times.

Everything is funny as long as it is happening to somebody else.

Will Rogers

I hate housework! You make the beds, you do the dishes - and six months later you have to start all over again.

Joan Rivers

We should not let our fears hold us back from pursuing our hopes.

John F. Kennedy

I don't care what is written about me so long as it isn't true.

Katharine Hepburn

Only one perfect woman ever existed - the woman your husband could have married.

Wrinkles should merely indicate where smiles have been.

Mark Twain

It is such a secret place, the land of tears.

Antoine de Saint-Exupery

There are no unimportant jobs, no unimportant people, no unimportant acts of kindness.

Unknown

I don't know anything about music. In my line you don't have to.

Elvis Presley

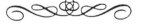

The height of misery is going up to the attic, reading your husband's old love letters and finding they're dated last week.

The most noble thing a man can inspire to, is charity.

George A. Brown

The difficult we do immediately: the impossible takes a little longer.

George Santayana

Whether it's the best of times, or the worst of times, it's the only time you've got.

Art Buchwald

They do not love that do not show their love.

William Shakespeare

Anybody who goes to see a psychiatrist ought to have his head examined.

Samuel Goldwyn

In America, alcohol is the only product people complain about when it works.

Stewart McIntosh

You shouldn't speak unless you can improve on the silence.

George A. Brown

If life was fair, Elvis would be alive and all the impersonators would be dead.

Johnny Carson

A man never discloses his own character so clearly as when he describes another's.

Jean Paul Richter

Good girls go to heaven and bad girls go everywhere.

At twenty years of age, the will reigns; at thirty, the wit; and at forty, the judgement.

Benjamin Franklin

I have a simple philosophy. Fill what's empty. Empty what's full. And scratch where it itches.

Alice Roosevelt Longworth

Invention is the mother of necessity.

Thorstein Veblen

Take time for all things: great haste makes great waste.

Benjamin Franklin

Happiness is when you see your husband's old girlfriend and she's fatter than you!

There's a sucker born every minute.

P. T. Barnum

It's what you learn after you know it all that counts.

John Wooden

If you think you can do a thing, or think you can't do a thing: Your right!

Henry Ford

Not to get what you have set your heart on is almost as bad as getting nothing at all.

Aristotle

When Jack Benny plays the violin, it sounds as if the strings are still back in the cat.

Fred Allen

The future will one day be the present and will seem as unimportant as the present does now.

W. Somerset Maugham

The manner of giving is worth more than the gift.

Pierre Corneille

Man is not the creature of circumstances. Circumstances are the creatures of men.

Benjamin Disraeli

Sometimes a scream is better than a thesis.

Ralph Waldo Emerson

Lead me not into temptation. I can find it by myself.

Dishonesty is like a boomerang. About the time you think all is well, it hits you in the back of the head.

Unknown

The best way to keep one's word is not to give it.

Napoleon I

Show me a man who cannot bother to do little things and I will show you a man who cannot be trusted to do big things.

Lawrence D. Bell

There should always be a time to think about thinking.

George A. Brown

You never really know a man until you have divorced him.

Zsa Zsa Gabor

Peace cannot be kept by force. It can only be achieved by understanding.

Albert Einstein

Procrastination is the thief of time.

Edward Young

It's futile to talk too much about the past...something like trying to make birth control retroactive.

Charles E. Wilson

After years of advising other people on their personal problems, I was stunned by my own divorce. I only wish I had someone to write to for help.

Ann Landers

It's not that I'm afraid to die. I just don't want to be there when it happens.

Woody Allen

Fortune and humour govern the world.

Francois de la Rochefoucauld

Money can buy you everything but happiness and pay your fare to every place but heaven.

Unknown

Here's the rule for bargains: "Do other men, for they would do you." That's the true business precept.

Charles Dickens

The really frightening thing about middle age is the knowledge that you'll grow out of it.

Doris Day

I know God will not give me anything I can't handle. I just wish that he didn't trust me so much.

Mother Teresa

Women are as old as they feel - and men are old when they lose their feelings.

Mae West

I've been on a calendar, but never on time.

Marilyn Monroe

Destiny is not a matter of chance; it is a matter if choice. It is not a thing to be waited for; it is a thing to be achieved.

William Jennings Bryan

Lord, what fools these mortals be!

William Shakespeare

I had a wonderful evening, but this wasn't it.

Groucho Marx

No one was ever so successful that they didn't appreciate a compliment.

George A. Brown

The people, and the people alone, are the motive force in the making of world history.

Mao Tse-Tung

We can be knowledgeable with other men's knowledge, but we cannot be wise with other men's wisdom.

Michel de Montaigne

A man who has not passed through the inferno of his passions has never overcome them.

Carl Jung

Behold the turtle - he makes progress only when he sticks his neck out!

I love my past. I love my present. I'm not ashamed of what I've had, and I'm not sad because I have it no longer.

Colette

A place for everything and everything in its place.

Isabella Mary Beeton

One fifth of the people are against everything all the time.

Robert F. Kennedy

You can't help getting older but you don't have to get old.

George Burns

Never insult an alligator until you've crossed the river.

Sometime they'll give a war and nobody will come.

Carl Sandburg

Necessity never made a good bargain.

Benjamin Franklin

When asked by an anthropologist what the Indians called America before the white man came, an Indian said simply, "Ours."

Vine Deloria, Jr.

I take a simple view of life: keep your eyes open and get on with it.

Laurence Olivier

When I was born I was so surprised I didn't talk for a year and a half.

Gracie Allen

Errors, like straws, upon the surface flow; He who would search for pearls must dive below.

John Dryden

Whoever is happy will make others happy too.

Anne Frank

The way to a man's heart is through his stomach.

Fanny Fern

What counts is not necessarily the size of the dog in the fight - it's the size of the fight in the dog.

Dwight D. Eisenhower

"You gave away my secret." "I did not, I exchanged it for another."

Let me assert my firm belief that the only thing we have to fear is fear itself.

Franklin D. Roosevelt

Regardless of what company you work for, never forget the most important product you're selling is yourself.

Unknown

Many men would take the death-sentence without a whimper to escape the life-sentence which fate carries in her other hand.

T.E. Lawrence

Sometimes it is better to have loved a little than to have loved a lot.

George A. Brown

Some men are attracted by a girl's mind. Others are attracted by what she doesn't mind.

Between two evils, I always pick the one I never tried before.

Mae West

I believe that our Heavenly Father invented man because he was disappointed in the monkey.

Mark Twain

Anger is never without a reason, but seldom a good one.

Benjamin Franklin

There are two ways of spreading light: to be the candle, or the mirror that reflects it.

Edith Wharton

If looks could kill, a lot of people would die with bridge cards in their hands.

We have seen better days.

William Shakespeare

Order marches with weighty and measured strides; disorder is always in a hurry.

Napoleon I

I make the most of all that comes and the least of all that goes.

Sara Teasdale

A first-rate organizer is never in a hurry. He is never late. He always keeps up his sleeve a margin for the unexpected.

Arnold Bennett

Please accept my resignation. I don't want to belong to any club that will accept me as a member.

Groucho Marx

Musicians don't retire; they stop when there's no more music in them.

Louis Armstrong

For years politicians have promised the moon. I'm the first one to be able to deliver it.

Richard Nixon

A crown is merely a hat that lets the rain in.

King Frederick the Great

We should take care not to make the intellect our god; it has, of course, powerful muscles, but no personality.

Albert Einstein

He has money to burn and she's a perfect match.

Give me the luxuries of life and I will willingly do without the necessities.

Frank Lloyd Wright

We are what and where we are, because we first imagined it.

George A.Brown

There's no sense in advertising your troubles - there's no market for them.

Unknown

Much more genius is needed to make love than to command armies.

Ninon de Lenclos

If it is such a small world, why does it cost so much to run it?

Don't be humble. You're not that great.

Golda Meir

There is nothing so consoling as to find that one's neighbour's troubles are at least as great as one's own.

George Moore

A fanatic is one who can't change his mind and won't change the subject.

Winston S. Churchill

I have not yet begun to fight.

John Paul Jones

A lot of women don't care who wears the pants in the family, as long as there is money in the pockets.

A sex symbol becomes a thing. I hate being a thing.

Marilyn Monroe

All animals are equal, but some animals are more equal than others.

George Orwell

Where the heart lies, let the brain lie also.

Robert Browning

Egotism is the anaesthetic that dulls the pain of stupidity.

Frank Leahy

To prevent a head cold from going to your chest, just tie a knot in your neck.

If only I had a little humility, I'd be perfect.

Ted Turner

I remember your name perfectly, but I just can't think of your face.

Rev. William Archibald Spooner

Just as courage imperils life, fear protects it.

Leonardo da Vinci

What's in a name? That which we call a rose...by any other name would smell as sweet.

William Shakespeare

Always get married early in the morning. That way, if it doesn't work out, you haven't wasted the whole day.

I will speak ill of no man, and speak all the good I know of everybody.

Benjamin Franklin

Knowledge which is acquired under compulsion obtains no hold on the mind.

Plato

I bet on a horse at ten to one. It didn't come in until half-past five.

Henny Youngman

What you get out of life is just interest on the repayment of the loan of what you have given.

George A. Brown

It's not a lie, it's a terminological inexactitude.

Alexander Haig

Laughter is a tranquillizer with no side effects.

Arnold Glasow

If you want to succeed you should strike out on new paths rather than travel the worn paths of accepted success.

John D. Rockefeller

To love oneself is the beginning of a life-long romance.

Oscar Wilde

You may be disappointed if you fail, but you are doomed if you don't try.

Beverly Sills

Dogs in Siberia are the fastest in the world, because the trees are so far apart.

Listen, everyone is entitled to my opinion.

Madonna

Beware of little expenses: a small leak will sink a ship.

Benjamin Franklin

If all economists were laid end to end, they would not reach a conclusion.

George Bernard Shaw

Pride makes us do things well. But it is love that makes us do them to perfection.

Unknown

I always do my best thinking over a glass of beer. Two heads are better than one.

Divorce is a game played by two lawyers.

Cary Grant

You can fool some of the people all the time and all the people some of the time; but you can't fool all the people all the time.

Abraham Lincoln

Nothing is easy to the unwilling.

Thomas Fuller

To lengthen thy life, lessen thy meals.

Benjamin Franklin

During last summer's heat wave, a local church put this on it's bulletin board. "You think it's hot here?"

We think women should have a choice when it comes to being pregnant. Barefoot is another story.

Kenneth Cole

You form a committee to study the matter, only when you don't want to react.

George A. Brown

I just put my feet in the air and move them around.

Fred Astaire

Courage is the price that life exacts for granting peace.

Amelia Earhart

Love is an itch around your heart that you can't scratch.

Complacency is the enemy of study. We cannot really learn anything until we rid ourselves of complacency.

Mao Tse-Tung

Dream what you dare to dream. Go where you want to go. Be what you want to be.

Calvin Coolidge

I don't even know what street Canada is on.

Al Capone

The customer is always right.

H. Gordon Selfridge

She tried to bake a birthday cake, but the candles melted in the oven.

Neither a borrower nor a lender be; For loan oft loses both itself and friend.

William Shakespeare

We make a living by what we get, but we make a life by what we give.

Winston S. Churchill

Every exit is an entry somewhere else.

Tom Stoppard

The things we know best are the things we haven't been taught.

Vauve Nargues

A verbal contract isn't worth the paper it's written on.

The royal road to a man's heart is to talk to him about the things he treasures most.

Dale Carnegie

A banker is a fellow who lends his umbrella when the sun is shining and wants it back the minute it begins to rain.

Mark Twain

The worker is the meat in the sandwich between the union and management and the union feeds off the worker and the management feeds the worker.

Adolf Hitler

A word to the wise ain't necessary - it's the stupid ones who need the advice.

Bill Cosby

If you obey all the rules, you miss all the fun.

Katharine Hepburn

Every advantage has its tax.

Ralph Waldo Emerson

To achieve great things we must live as though we were never going to die.

Marquis de Vauvenargues

In a word, I am always busy, which is perhaps the chief reason why I am always well.

Elizabeth Cady Stanton

The essence of life is to live long without growing old.

George A. Brown

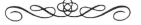

You only live once, and if you play it right, once is all you need.

Joe E. Lewis

Those who dare to fail miserably can achieve greatly.

Robert F. Kennedy

The dinosaur's eloquent lesson is that if some bigness is good, an overabundance of bigness is not necessarily better.

Eric Johnson

England is the paradise of individuality, eccentricity, heresy, anomalies, hobbies, and humours.

George Santayana

Only a mediocre man is always at his best.

W. Somerset Maugham

It is not true that life is one damn thing after another - it's one damn thing over and over.

Edna St. Vincent Millay

Only those who have learned the power of sincere and selfless contribution experience life's deepest joy - true fulfillment.

Anthony Robbins

He that won't be counselled can't be helped.

Benjamin Franklin

Most of us hate to see a poor loser or a rich winner.

Harold Coffin

Heroes are the people who do what needs to be done regardless of the consequences.

George A. Brown

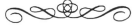

My wife ran off with my best friend, and I still miss him a lot.

Variety's the very spice of life, that gives it all its flavour.

Cowper

Show me a person who has never made a mistake and I'll show you somebody who has never achieved much.

Joan Collins

When you tell the truth, you never have to worry about your lousy memory.

Unknown

I never forget a face, but I'll make an exception in your case.

Groucho Marx

When life hands you a lemon - make lemonade!

The art of medicine consists of amusing the patient while Nature cures the disease.

Voltaire

Youth is a blunder; manhood a struggle; old age a regret.

Benjamin Disraeli

Ninety percent of the friction of life is caused by the wrong tone of voice.

Unknown

No legacy is so rich as honesty.

William Shakespeare

I'm stubborn only when I don't get my way.

Selfishness is not living as one wishes to live. It is asking others to live as one wishes to live.

Macaulay

Fate leads the willing, and drags along the reluctant.

Seneca

It is a wise father that knows his own child.

William Shakespeare

Aviation is proof that, given the will, we have the capacity to achieve the impossible.

Eddie Rickenbacker

I'm not young enough to know everything.

The winds and waves are always on the side of the ablest navigators.

Edward Gibbon

The reward of a thing well done is to have done it.

Ralph Waldo Emerson

Maturity is realizing that your parents were not always right.

George A. Brown

If you want work well done, select a busy man: the other kind has no time.

Elbert Hubbard

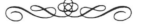

If you think English is an easy language to learn, then how is it "Fat Chance" means the same as "Slim Chance".

The German people is no warlike nation. It is a soldierly one, which means it does not want war but does not fear war. It loves peace but it also loves its honour and freedom.

Adolf Hitler

Life is either a daring adventure, or nothing.

Helen Keller

A group of two hundred executives were asked what makes a person successful. Eighty percent listed enthusiasm as the most important quality.

Unknown

Please all and you will please none.

Aesop

When buying a cold remedy, always buy the cheapest - the expensive ones don't work either!

You can't hold a man down without staying down with him.

Booker T. Washington

In the game of life even the 50-yard line seats don't interest me. I came to play.

Unknown

We stand today on the edge of a new frontier.

John F. Kennedy

Believe me, you have to get up early if you want to get out of bed.

Groucho Marx

Too much of a good thing is wonderful!

The more things change, the more they remain the same.

Alphonse Karr

Come up and see me sometime.

Mae West

One sword keeps another in the sheath.

George Herbert

The mass of men lead lives of quiet desperation.

Henry David Thoreau

At first I was hesitant - but now, I'm not so sure.

You should fill your life with experiences ... not excuses.

George A. Brown

Time is the greatest innovator.

Francis Bacon

The lion and the calf shall lie down together but the calf won't get much sleep.

Woody Allen

Never bet on baseball.

Pete Rose

There's nothing wrong with teenagers that reasoning won't aggravate!

The only limit to our realization of tomorrow will be our doubts of today.

Franklin D. Roosevelt

It is only a step from the sublime to the ridiculous.

Napoleon I

Happy is he who learns to bear what he cannot change!

Johann Friedrich von Schiller

Nothing great was ever achieved without enthusiasm.

Ralph Waldo Emerson

Cat hair adheres to everything - but the cat.

A strong foe is better than a weak friend.

Edward Dahlberg

Imagination is the highest kite one can fly.

Lauren Bacall

You never get a second chance to make a good first impression.

Unknown

From each according to his abilities, to each according to his needs.

Karl Marx

Whenever I meet a man who would make a good husband - he is.

Political power grows out of the barrel of a gun.

Mao Tse-Tung

Ninety-eight percent of the adults in this country are decent, hard-working, honest Americans. It's the other lousy two percent that get all the publicity. But then, we elected them.

Lily Tomlin

To know how to grow old is the master work of wisdom, and one of the most difficult chapters in the great art of living.

Henri F. Amiel

Not in time, place or circumstance, but in the man lies success.

Charles Rouce

In a thousand years we shall all forget the things that trouble us now.

Adam Lindsay Gordon

Nothing happens unless first a dream.

Carl Sandsurg

The man who wins may have been counted out several times, but he didn't hear the referee.

H. E. Jansen

Push, pull or get out of the way.

George A. Brown

Father, I cannot tell a lie. I did it with my hatchet.

George Washington

To err is human, but to blame it on someone else is humaner.

Always be a little kinder than necessary.

James M. Barrie

Don't carry a grudge. While you're carrying the grudge the other guy's out dancing.

Buddy Hackett

I'm not against the police, I'm just afraid of them.

Alfred Hitchcock

People are easily anaesthetized by overstatement, and there is a danger that the environmental movement will fall flat on its face when it is most needed, simply because it has pitched its tale too strongly.

John Maddox

You have two choices for dinner - take it or leave it!

Nothing splendid has ever been achieved except by those who dared believed that something inside of them was superior to the circumstances.

Bruce Barton

If we all did the things we are capable of doing, we would literally astound ourselves.

Thomas A. Edison

It is in your moments of decision that your destiny is shaped.

Anthony Robbins

Be more concerned with your character than your reputation, because your character is what you really are, while your reputation is merely what others think you are.

John Wooden

It's always good to lend a sympathetic ear, but sometimes it's hard to get it back.

When small men attempt great enterprises, they always end by reducing them to the level of their mediocrity.

Napoleon 1

It's not how far you fall, but how high you bounce.

Unknown

Recipe For Greatness - To bear up under loss; To fight the bitterness of defeat and the weakness of grief; To be victor over anger; To smile when tears are close; To resist disease and evil men and base instincts; To hate hate and to love love; To go on when it would seem good to die; To look up with unquenchable faith in something ever more about to be. That is what any man can do, and be great.

Zane Grey

Hold yourself responsible for a higher standard than anybody expects of you.

Henry Wary Beechel

I've been in hot water so often I feel like a tea bag.

I know of no more encouraging fact than the unquestionable ability of man to elevate his life by a conscious elevator.

Henry David Thoreau

I am part of all that I have met.

Alfred Lord Tennyson

I am not discouraged, because every wrong attempt is another step forward.

Thomas Edison

A wealthy person is the one content with himself.

George A. Brown

If you want to be seen, stand up
If you want to be heard, speak up
If you want to be appreciated - sit down and shut up!

The manager administers, the leader innovates.
The manager maintains, the leader develops.
The manager relies on systems, the leader relies on people.
The manager counts on controls, the leader counts on trust.
The manager does things right, the leader does the right thing.

Fortune Magazine

We will either find a way, or make one.

Hannibal

You can't think and hit at the same time.

Yogi Berra

Failure is success if we learn from it.

Malcomb S. Forbes

A boy is grown when he'd rather steal a kiss than second base.

The only gracious way to accept an insult is to ignore it: if you can't ignore it, top it: if you can't top it, laugh at it: if you can't laugh at it, it's probably deserved.

Russell Lynes

Forgive and forget. Sour grapes make for a lousy wine.

Unknown

I don't say we all ought to misbehave, but we ought to look as if we could.

Orson Wells

Men live by intervals of reason under the sovereignty of humour and passion.

Sir Thomas Brown

A man usually feels better after a few winks, especially if she winks back.

Men as well as women, are much oftener led by their hearts than by their understandings.

Lord Chesterfield

Creative minds always have been known to survive any kind of bad training.

Anna Freud

The secret of success is learning how to use pain and pleasure instead of having pain and pleasure use you. If you do that your in control of your life, if you don't, life controls you.

Anthony Robbins

The unknown is an ocean. What is conscience? The compass of the unknown.

Joseph Cook

I once missed a hole in one by only five strokes.

The three most important words in the English lanuage are: "Are you okay?"

George A. Brown

If you judge people, you have no time to love them.

Mother Teresa

Don't be afraid to take big steps.   You can't cross a chasm in two small jumps.

David Lloyd George

When the One Great Scorer comes to write against your name, He marks, not that you won or lost, but how you played the game.

Grantland Rice

We've been through a lot together and most of it is your fault.

Challenges can be stepping stones or stumbling blocks. It's just a matter of how you view them.

Unknown

Don't let what you cannot do interfere with what you can do.

John Wooden

Winning is not a sometime thing; it's an all-time thing. You don't win once in a while, you don't do things right once in a while, you do them right all the time. Winning is a habit. Unfortunately, so is losing.

Vince Lombardi

Prefer a loss to a dishonest gain; the one brings pain at the moment, the other for all time.

Chilton

Behind every successful man stands a proud wife and surprised mother-in-law.

Brooks Hays

In the middle of difficulty lies opportunity.

Albert Einstein

I'd rather hit than have sex.

Reggie Jackson

The essence of being human is that one does not seek perfection.

George Orwell

Make new friends, but keep the old; the first are silver the latter, gold.

Unknown

When I'm good, I'm very good, but when I'm bad, I'm better.

Mae West

It's far easier to forgive an enemy after you've got even with him.

Olin Miller

Two stonecutters were asked what they were doing. The first said, "I'm cutting this stone into blocks." The second replied, "I'm on a team that's building a cathedral."

Old Story

To travel hopefully is better than to arrive.

Sir James Jeans

When an old person dies, a library is lost.

Tommy Swann

Don't be too fussy, girls. There are women who waited so long for their ship to come in, their pier collapsed.

The halls of fame are open wide and they are always full. Some go in by the door called push and some by the door called pull.

Stanley Baldwin

Women who seek to be equal with men lack ambition.

Timothy Leary

One man's poison is another man's drug.

Ronald Knox

When you were born, you cried and the world rejoiced. Live your life in such a manner that when you die the world cries and you rejoice.

Old Indian saying

*My wife made UFO's yesterday - Unidentified **frying** objects.*

We must all hang together or assuredly we shall all hang separately.

Benjamin Franklin

The harder I work, the luckier I get.

Samuel Goldwyn

Everyone can afford praise. It costs the least.

George A. Brown

Find a collaborator, like Ben and Jerry and the Wright brothers did.

Unknown

I was trying to get a new car for my wife but no one would swap.

There is nothing like dreams to create the future.

Victor Hugo

Nature has placed mankind under the government of two sovereign masters, pain and pleasure. They govern us in all we do, in all we say, in all we think, every effort we can make to throw off our subjection, will serve but to demonstrate and confirm it.

Jeremy Bentham

A strong code of ethics is as reliable as a compass.

Unknown

Society may predict, but only I will determine my destiny.

Marva Collins

"Where does virgin wool come from?"
"From sheep that run the fastest."

The toughest thing about success is that you've got to keep on being a success.

Irving Berlin

What hunger is in relation to food, zest is in relation to life.

Bertrand Russell

I find television very educational. Every time someone switches it on I go into another room and read a good book.

Groucho Marx

Big Brother is watching you.

George Orwell

Next to hot chicken soup, a tattoo of an anchor on your chest, and penicillin, I consider a honeymoon one of the most overrated events in the world.

Erma Bombeck

I will make you shorter by a head.

Elizabeth 1 of England

There are two kinds of women: those who want power in the world, and those who want power in bed.

Jacqueline Kennedy Onassis

The hardest thing in the world to understand is income tax.

Albert Einstein

The only place success comes before work is in a dictionary.

Vidal Sassoon

It's going to be fun to watch and see how long the meek can keep the earth after they inherit it.

Frank McKinney Hubbard

Hitch your wagon to a star.

Ralph Waldo Emerson

Zest is the secret of all beauty. There is no beauty that is attractive without zest.

Christian Dior

Things do not change, we change.

Henry Dave Thoreau

If a man with money meets a man with experience, the man with experience ends up with the money and the man with the money ends up with experience.

George A. Brown

The meek shall inherit the earth but not the mineral rights.

J. Paul Getty

Seeing is believing but feeling's the truth.

Thomas Fuller M.D.

The biggest mistake you can make is to believe that you work for someone else.

Unknown

There never was a good war or a bad peace.

Benjamin Franklin

In a full heart there is room for everything, and in a empty heart there is room for nothing.

Antonio Porchia

The poor wish to be rich, the rich wish to be happy, the single wish to be married, and the married wish to be dead.

Ann Landers

Everybody talks about the weather, but nobody does anything about it.

Charles Dudley Warner

Don't fire until you see the whites of their eyes.

William Prescott

A wife must be a chef in the kitchen, a hostess in the dining room and a hooker in bed.

Unknown

If you knew how meat was made, you'd probably lose your lunch. I know - I'm from cattle country. That's why I became a vegetarian.

K. D. Lang

The difference between the right word and the almost right word is the difference between lightning and the lightning bug.

Mark Twain

The only reward of virtue is virtue; the only way to have a friend is to be one.

Ralph Waldo Emerson

Do not take life too seriously. You will never get out of it alive.

Elbert Hubbard

Some rise by sin, and some by virtue fall.

William Shakespeare

Husbands are chiefly good lovers when they are betraying their wives.

Marilyn Monroe

Let us swear while we may, for in heaven it will not be allowed.

Mark Twain

A man who wants to lead the orchestra must turn his back on the crowd.

James Crook

Television has proved that people will look at anything rather than at each other.

Ann Landers

The two most important ingredients in a relationship are **courtesy** and **respect**. Over time, they are the two that cannot be pretended.

George A. Brown

I love being a writer. What I can't stand is the paperwork.

Peter De Vries

The great question...which I have not been able to answer, despite my thirty years of research into the feminine soul, is "What does a woman want?"

Sigmund Freud

A real friend will tell you your faults and follies in times of prosperity, and assist you with his hand and heart in times of adversity.

Unknown

Winning isn't everything, but wanting to win is.

Vince Lombardi

I don't know, I don't care, and it doesn't make any difference.

Jack Kerouac

A hair perhaps divides the False and True.

Omar Khayyam

If truth is beauty, how come no one has their hair done in a library?

Lily Tomlin

Truth lives on in the midst of deception.

Adrienne Rich

Wealth is the product of man's capacity to think.

Ayn Rand

God will not look you over for medals, degrees or diplomas, but for scars!

Elbert Hubbard

Never look down on anybody unless you're helping them up.

Jesse Jackson

When you get to the end of your rope, tie a knot and hang on.

Franklin D. Roosevelt

He who can, does. He who cannot, teaches.

George Bernard Shaw

What is written without effort is in general read without pleasure.

Samuel Johnson

Many people would sooner die than think. In fact they do.

Bertrand Russell

Thoughts are energy. And you can make your world or break your world by thinking.

Susan Taylor

I've got two reasons for success and I'm standing on both of them.

Betty Grable

Style is the mind skating circles round itself as it moves forward.

Robert Frost

Only little people pay taxes.

Leona Helmsley

The play was a great success, but the audience was a disaster.

Oscar Wilde

To have a peace of mind that passes your judgement is wealth beyond belief.

George A. Brown

I generally avoid temptation unless I can't resist it.

Mae West

People are more influenced by how much I care, than by how much I know.

Unknown

I don't think there are any men who are faithful to their wives.

Jacqueline Kennedy Onassis

A house divided against itself cannot stand.

Abraham Lincoln

The vigorous are no better than the lazy during one half of life, for all men are alike when asleep.

Aristotle

First you forget names, then you forget faces, then you forget to pull your zipper up, then you forget to pull your zipper down.

Leo Rosenburg

You know I hate fighting. If I knew how to make a living some other way, I would.

Muhammad Ali

I'd rather have a first class manager run a second rate business than a second class manager run a first class business.

Jack E. Reichert

Traditionalists are pessimists about the future and optimists about the past.

Lewis Mumford

Style is primarily a matter of instinct.

Bill Blass

If hospitals are places to get well, why do they serve plastic food?

The ballot is stronger than the bullet.

Abraham Lincoln

The shortest distance between two people is a smile.

Victor Borge

Every moment is a golden one for him who has the vision to recognize it as such.

Henry Miller

You can lead a horse to water but you can't make him drink.

Unknown

A wise man never laughs at his wife's old clothes.

Intelligence is quickness in seeing things as they really are.

George Santayana

The wise man, even when he holds his tongue, says more than the fool when he speaks.

Thomas Fuller

I came, I saw, I conquered.

Julius Caesar

An injury is much sooner forgotten than an insult.

Earl of Chesterfield

Wishing without work is like fishing without bait.

Frank Tyger

We cannot always build the future for our youth, but we can build our youth for the future.

Franklin D. Roosevelt

Diligence is the mother of good luck.

Benjamin Franklin

Get someone else to blow your horn and the sound will carry twice as far.

Will Rodgers

No man sees far, the most see no farther than their noses.

Thomas Carlyle

A philosopher is a person who knows just what to do ... until it happens to him.

Do what you can, with what you have, where you are.

Theodore Roosevelt

To the dull mind all nature is leaden. To the illumined mind the whole world burns and sparkles with light.

Ralph Waldo Emerson

Our thoughts determine our responses to life. We are not victims of the world. To the extent that we control our thoughts, we control the world.

Unknown

At no time is freedom of speech more precious than when a man hits his thumb with a hammer.

Marshall Lumsaden

I can't be overdrawn ... I still have cheques.

The purpose of learning is growth, and our minds, unlike our bodies, can continue growing as we continue to live.

Mortimer Adler

People are always ready to admit a man's ability after he gets there.

Bob Edwards

Research is to see what everybody else has seen, and to think what nobody else has thought.

Albert Szent-Gyorgyi

Kind hearts are the garden.
Kind thoughts are the roots
Kind words are the blossoms
Kind deeds are the fruits.

John Ruskin

The best substitute for experience is being sixteen.

Raymond Duncan

If you are going to be sorry, be sorry for the things you've done - not the things you haven't done. Don't wait to get to the rocking chair to say - if only.

George A. Brown

History is the record of an encounter between character and circumstance.

Donald Creighton

We cherish our friends not for their ability to amuse us, but for ours to amuse them.

Evelyn Waugh

You can't sit on the lid of progress. If you do, you will be blown to pieces.

Henry J. Kaiser

I have the most frustrated pet in the world - a turtle that chases cars!

Man - a creature made at the end of the week's work when God was tired.

Mark Twain

To treat your facts with imagination is one thing, but to imagine your facts is another.

John Burroughs

People who take time to be alone usually have depth, originality, and quiet reserve.

John Miller

Nearly all men can stand adversity, but if you want to test a man's character, give him power.

Abraham Lincoln

I know a golfer that cheats so much, when he got a hole-in-one, he wrote a zero on his score card.

We all worry about the population explosion - but we don't worry about it at the right time.

Arthur Hoppe

Anybody can be Pope; the proof of this is that I have become one.

Pope John XXIII

Life is like playing a violin in public and learning the instrument as one goes on.

Samuel Butler

The smallest act of kindness is worth more than the grandest intention.

Unknown

Success is simply a matter of luck. Ask any failure.

Earl Wilson

Nobody has a more sacred obligation to obey the law than those who make the law.

Sophocles

A man who has never gone to school may steal from a freight car; but if he has a university education, he may steal the whole railroad.

Theodore Roosevelt

The more a child feels valued, the better his values will be.

George A. Brown

Work is achieved by those employees who have not yet reached their level of incompetence.

Laurence J. Peter

Don't knock the rich. When did a poor person give you a job?

Laurence J. Peter

The finest steel has to go through the hottest fire.

Richard M. Nixon

We live in a society where the sin is getting caught.

Anna Mary (Grandma Moses)

It takes a great man to make a good listener.

Sir Arthur Helps

Little things affect little minds.

Benjamin Disraeli

The trick is to make sure you don't die waiting for prosperity to come.

Lee Iacocca

We have citizens enough to be prosperous had we not so many politicians.

Merv F. Thurgood

I have spoken. You have heard; you know the facts; now give your decision.

Aristotle

I know but one freedom and that is the freedom of the mind.

Antoine de Saint-Exupery

Wars may be fought with weapons .... but they are won by men.

Unknown

Lady Astor:
> *Winston, if you were my husband, I should flavour your coffee with poison.*
Winston Churchill:
> *Madam, if I were your husband, I should drink it.*
> *Winston S. Churchill*

There is this difference between happiness and wisdom; he that thinks himself the happiest man really is so; but he that thinks himself the wisest, is generally the greatest fool.

Colton

Impossible is a word only to be found in the dictionary of fools.

Napoleon I

The bird of paradise alights only upon the hand that does not grasp.

John Berry

Procrastination is the thief of time.

D. Young

The only time a woman wishes she were a year older is when she is expecting a baby.

Mary Marsh

He who reigns within himself, and rules passions, desires and fears, is more than a king.

Milton

Men are born with two eyes, but with one tongue, in order that they should see twice as much as they say.

Colton

Impersonal criticism is like an impersonal fist fight or an impersonal marriage, and as successful.

George Jean Nathan

No one man can terrorize a whole nation unless we are all his accomplices.

Edward R. Murrow

People who are smart, industrious, kind, honest and likeable just seem to have all the luck.

Men will sooner surrender their rights than their customs.

Moritz Guedemann

Diplomacy: The art of jumping into troubled waters without making a splash.

Art Linkletter

Nothing is so soothing to our self-esteem as to find our bad traits in our forbearers. It seems to absolve us.

Van Wyck Brooks

The greatest lesson in life is to know that even fools are right sometimes.

Winston S. Churchill

Man blames fate for other accidents, but feels personally responsible when he makes a hole in one.

Horizons Magazine

The main thing needed to make men happy is intelligence ... and it can be fostered by education.

Bertrand Russell

The defect of equality is that we only desire it with our superiors.

Henry Becque

In an argument with your spouse, the first one to say I'm sorry is the winner.

George A. Brown

Every man's memory is his private literature.

Aldous Huxley

A woman drove me to drink and I never even had the courtesy to thank her.

W. C. Fields

It isn't that we can't see the solution. It is that they can't see the problem.

G. K. Chesterton

Every great man of business has got somewhere a touch of the idealist in him.

Woodrow Wilson

Nothing fixes a thing so intensely in the memory as the wish to forget it.

Michel de Montaigne

Most of us believe in trying to make other people happy only if they can be happy in ways which we approve.

Robert S. Lynd

The only really happy folk are married women and single men.

H. L. Mencken

We would often be ashamed of our finest actions if the world understood all the motives which produced them.

Duc de La Rochefoucauld

It is never too late to give up your prejudices.

Henry David Thoreau

I am not afraid of tomorrow, for I have seen yesterday and I love today.

William Allen White

Men just don't seem to jump off the bridge for big reasons; they usually do so for little ones.

W. H. Ferry

When you see yourself quoted in print and you're sorry you said it, it suddenly becomes a misquotation.

Laurence J. Peter

A diplomat is a man who always remembers a woman's birthday but never remembers her age.

Robert Frost

Absence makes the heart grow fonder.

Thomas Haynes Bayly

Ignorance of the law does not prevent the losing lawyer from collecting his bill.

Puck Magazine

Any political party which takes credit for the rain must not be surprised if its opponents blame it for the drought.

Dwight W. Morrow

Grandmother rode in a horse-drawn carriage, but was afraid to ride in an automobile.
Her daughter rode in an automobile, but was afraid to ride in an aeroplane.
Her grand-daughter travels in a jet aeroplane, but would be afraid to ride in a horse-drawn carriage.

They shall not grow old, as we that are left grow old; age shall not weary them, nor the years condemn. At the going down of the sun and in the morning we will remember them. Lest we forget.

Unknown

It is impossible to teach without learning.

George A. Brown

Life does not cease to be funny when people die, any more than it ceases to be serious when people laugh.

George Bernard Shaw

A little learning is not a dangerous thing to one who does not mistake it for a great deal.

William Allen White

I always keep a supply of stimulant handy in case I see a snake -- which I also keep handy.

W. C. Fields

Sixty years ago I knew everything; now I know nothing; education is a progressive discovery of our own ignorance.

Will Durant

The more alternatives, the more difficult the choice.

Abbe D'Allainval

That's one small step for a man, one giant leap for mankind.

Neil Armstrong

Virtue is like a rich stone, best plain set.

Francis Bacon

Advice is what we ask for when we already know the answer but wish we didn't.

Erica Jong

The ultimate censorship is the flick of the dial.

Tom Smothers

History is the ship carrying living memories to the future.

Stephen Spender

When people are serving, life is no longer meaningless.

John Gardner

It is easy to be tolerant of the principles of other people if you have none of your own.

Sir Herbert Samuel

There are three things I always forget. Names, faces - and the third I can't remember.

Italo Svevo

Human affairs are not serious, but they have to be taken seriously.

John Cougar Mellencamp

When a man assumes a public trust, he should consider himself as public property.

Thomas Jefferson

To be a success in business, be daring, be first, be different.

Marchant

Every new opinion, at its starting, is precisely in a minority of one.

Thomas Carlyle

When all else fails, lower your standards.

George A. Brown

There is nothing more demoralizing than a small but adequate income.

Edmund Wilson

The same people who can deny others everything are famous for refusing themselves nothing.

Leigh Hunt

A jury too often has at least one member who is more ready to hang the panel than the traitor.

Abraham Lincoln

Feeling good gets better when it is shared.

George A. Brown

"My husband is so possessive that he refers to our wedding album as his owner's manual."

Prejudice is a matter of being down on something you're not up on.

Unknown

To read without reflecting is like eating without digesting.

Edmund Burke

What men value in this world is not rights but privileges.

H. L. Mencken

The things taught in schools and colleges are not an education, but the means of education.

Ralph Waldo Emerson

I've learned the quickest way to meet people is to pick up the wrong golf ball on the golf course.

Business without profit is not business any more than a pickle is a candy.

Charles F. Abbott

Always remember others may hate you but those who hate you don't win unless you hate them. And then you destroy yourself.

Richard M. Nixon

The great pleasure in life is doing what people say you cannot do.

Walter Bagehot

A problem well stated is a problem half solved.

Charles F. Kettering

I'm a practising heterosexual ... but bisexuality immediately doubles your chances for a date on Saturday night.

Woody Allen

There is something that is much more scarce, something rarer than ability. It is the ability to recognize ability.

Robert Half

Only the young die good.

Oliver Herford

Leadership is **action**, not position.

Donald H. McGannon

To limit the press is to insult a nation; to prohibit reading of certain books is to declare the inhabitants to be either fools or slaves.

Claude A. Helvetius

What every house needs is more shelves.

George A. Brown

If we are not ashamed to think it, we should not be ashamed to say it.

Marcus Tullius Cicero

Men ... employ speech only to conceal their thoughts.

Voltaire

There is no such thing as a moral or an immoral book. Books are well written or badly written.

Oscar Wilde

You have not lost until you quit.

Eugene G. Ursual

Ask not what you can do for your country, for they are liable to tell you.

Mark Steinbeck

A man who dares to waste one hour of time has not discovered the value of life.

Charles Darwin

There's a mighty big difference between good, sound reasons and reasons that sound good.

Burton Hillis

The measure of a man's real character is what he would do if he knew he never would be found out.

Thomas Babington Macaulay

Everybody is ignorant, only on different subjects.

Will Rogers

The hardest to convince they're at the retirement age are children at bedtime.

Shannon Fife

A free society is one where it is safe to be unpopular.

Adlai Stevenson

Creativeness often consists of merely turning up what is already there. Did you know that right and left shoes were thought up only a little more than a century ago?

Bernice Fitz-Gibbon

When the white man came we had the land and they had the Bibles; now they have the land and we have the Bibles.

Chief Dan George

If you would not be forgotten as soon as you are dead, either write things worth reading or do things worth writing.

Benjamin Franklin

If life were fair - there would be no need for salads.

One of my chief regrets during my years in the theatre is that I couldn't sit in the audience and watch me.

John Barrymore

You won't fall off the bicycle unless you quit peddling.

David H. Blair

The chief object of education is not to learn things but to unlearn things.

G. K. Chesterton

Experience is the worst teacher; it gives the test before presenting the lesson.

Vernon Law

I'm glad I don't have to explain to a man from Mars why each day I set fire to dozens of little pieces of paper, and then put them in my mouth.

Mignon McLaughlin

A government that robs Peter to pay Paul can always depend upon the support of Paul.

George Bernard Shaw

Planned obsolescence is another word for progress.

James Jeffrey Roche

An intellectual is a man who takes more words than necessary to tell more than he knows.

Dwight D. Eisenhower

There is only one quality worse than hardness of heart and that is softness of head.

Theodore Roosevelt

The cost of living has gone up another dollar a quart.

W. C. Fields

The tragedy of life is what dies inside a man while he lives.

Albert Schweitzer

We need to make a world in which fewer children are born, and in which we take better care of them.

Dr. George Wald

The essence of true friendship is to make allowance for another's little lapses.

David Storey

The things that are wrong with the country today are the sum total of all the things that are wrong with us as individuals.

Charles W. Tobey

I've known what it is to be hungry, but I always went right to a restaurant.

Ring Lardner

The middle of the road is where the white line is ... and that's the worst place to drive.

Robert Frost

Equality of opportunity is an equal opportunity to prove unequal talents.

Sir Herbert Samuel

There is just one thing I can promise you about the outer-space program: Your tax dollar will go farther.

Wernher von Braun

If you care, it shows. If you don't care, it shows more.

George A. Brown

Teenager: Fooling my mom is like trying to sneak a sunrise past a rooster.

God gave us memory that we might have roses in December.

James M. Barrie

News is the first rough draft of history.

Ben Bradlee

No man knows his true character until he has run out of gas, purchased something on the installment plan and raised an adolescent.

Mercelene Cox

It's the most unhappy people who most fear change.

Mignon McLaughlin

We lived for days on nothing but food and water.

W. C. Fields

Human action can be modified to some extent, but human nature cannot be changed.

Abraham Lincoln

Dishonesty is like a boomerang. About the time you think all is well, it hits you in the back of the head.

Unknown

People have one thing in common: they are all different.

Robert Zend

If you cannot get rid of the family skeleton, make it dance.

Harry S. Truman

A fool and his money are soon parted. The rest of us wait to be taxed.

There is no stigma attached to recognizing a bad decision in time to install a better one.

Laurence J. Peter

As I would not be a slave, so I would not be a master. This expresses my idea of democracy.

Abraham Lincoln

We must respect the other fellow's religion, but only in the same sense and to the extent that we respect his theory that his wife is beautiful and his children smart.

H. L. Mencken

Why does a woman work ten years to change a man's habits and then complain that he's not the man she married?

Barbra Streisand

She got her good looks from her father ... he's a plastic surgeon.

Groucho Marx

Science without religion is lame, religion without science is blind.

Albert Einstein

Every man has three characters ... that which he exhibits, that which he has, and that which he thinks he has.

Alphonse Karr

The road to Hell is paved with good intentions.

Samuel Johnson

It is easier to fight for one's principles than to live up to them.

Alfred Adler

Oh, to be only half as wonderful as my child thought I was when he was small, and only half as stupid as my teen-ager now thinks I am.

Rebecca Richards

A speech is a solemn responsibility. The man who makes a bad thirty-minute speech to two hundred people wastes only a half hour of his own time but he wastes one hundred hours of the audience's time ... more than four days ... which should be a hanging offense.

Jenkin Lloyd Jones

Adam was the only man who, when he said a good thing, knew that nobody had said it before him.

Mark Twain

Logic is an instrument used for bolstering a prejudice.

Elbert Hubbard

No extraordinary power should be lodged in any one individual.

George Bernard Shaw

Many a dumb blonde is really a smart brunette.

Nothing is easier than spending public money. It does not appear to belong to anybody. The temptation is overwhelming to bestow it on somebody.

Calvin Coolidge

As I grow older, I pay less attention to what men say. I just watch what they do.

Andrew Carnegie

You can catch more flies with honey than you can with a hammer.

George A. Brown

We do our best that we know how at the moment, and if it doesn't turn out, we modify it.

Franklin D. Roosevelt

A diplomat is a person who can tell you to go to hell in such a way that you actually look forward to the trip.

Caskie Stinnett

But I have seen the science I worshipped and the aircraft I loved destroying the civilization I expected them to serve.

Charles A. Lindbergh, Jr.

The worst misfortune that can happen to an ordinary man is to have an extraordinary father.

Austin O'Malley

There's only one thing that can keep growing without nourishment: the human ego.

Marshall Lumsden

A banker is a person who is willing to make a loan if you present sufficient evidence to show you don't need it.

Herbert V. Prochnow

Most of us spend the first six days of each week sowing wild oats, then we go to church on Sunday and pray for a crop failure.

Fred Allen

Treat people as if they were what they ought to be and you help them to become what they are capable of being.

Johann W. von Goethe

I'd be astounded if this planet is still going fifty years from now. I don't think we will reach 2000. It would be miraculous.

Alistair Cooke

I don't like to commit myself about heaven and hell .. you see, I have friends in both places.

Mark Twain

Millions long for immortality who do not know what to do with themselves on a rainy Sunday afternoon.

Susan Ertz

When I was a kid I said to my father one afternoon, "Daddy, will you take me to the zoo?" He answered, "If the zoo wants you let them come and get you."

Jerry Lewis

One thing you will probably remember well is any time you forgive and forget.

Franklin P. Jones

The difference between intelligence and education is this: intelligence will make you a good living.

Charles F. Kettering

It is better to deserve honours and not have them than to have them and not deserve them.

Mark Twain

If the shoe fits, you're not allowing for growth.

Robert N. Coons

It's possible to own too much. A man with one watch knows what time it is; a man with two watches is never quite sure.

Lee Segall

The principal mark of genius is not perfection but originality, the opening of new frontiers.

Arthur Koestler

I don't know who my grandfather was; I am much more concerned to know what his grandson will be.

Abraham Lincoln

True friendship is like sound health, the value of it is seldom known until it be lost.

Charles Caleb Colton

If you look for the worst in people you will find it. If you look for the best you will find it much more rewarding.

George A. Brown

I used to be Snow White.........but I drifted.

Mae West

To get profit without risk, experience without danger, and reward without work, is as impossible as it is to live without being born.

A. P. Gouthey

As you get older, fight only the battles that you can win. It helps the confidence level.

George A. Brown

I'm a great believer in luck, and I find the harder I work the more I have of it.

Thomas Jefferson

No man is fit to command another that cannot command himself.

William Penn

Middle age is when your old classmates are so grey and wrinkled and bald they don't recognize you.

Bennett Cerf

The fact that people do not understand and respect the very best things, such as Mozart's concertos, is what permits men like us to become famous.

Johannes Brahms

Democracy is a device that insures we shall be governed no better than we deserve.

George Bernard Shaw

Progress is a nice word but change is its motivator and change has its enemies.

Robert F. Kennedy

Another good reducing exercise consists in placing both hands against the table edge and pushing back.

Robert Quillen

You know you're getting old when the candles cost more than the cake.

Bob Hope

Since we cannot know all that is to be known of everything, we ought to know a little about everything.

Blaise Pascal

The most valuable of all talents is that of never using two words when one will do.

Thomas Jefferson

Fame creates its own standards. A guy who twitches his lips is just another guy with a lip twitch ... unless he's Humphrey Bogart.

Sammy Davis, Jr.

A man's reputation is the opinion people have of him; his character is what he really is.

Jack Miner

The trouble with being punctual is that nobody's there to appreciate it.

Franklin P. Jones

I would rather be an opportunist and float than go to the bottom with my principles around my neck.

Stanley Baldwin

It took me fifteen years to discover I had no talent for writing, but I couldn't give it up because by that time I was too famous.

Robert Benchley

I have nothing to hide. The White House has nothing to hide.

Richard M. Nixon

Position can be bought....respect must be earned.

George A. Brown

Statistics are like a bikini. What they reveal is suggestive, but what they conceal is vital.

Aaron Levenstein

Those who expect to reap the blessings of freedom must, like men, undergo the fatigue of supporting it.

Thomas Paine

A person's own good manners are the best security against the rudeness of others.

Unknown

Time: that which man is always trying to kill, but which ends in killing him.

Herbert Spencer

I'd rather wake up in the middle of nowhere than in any city on earth.

Steve McQueen

When I was forty, my doctor advised me that a man in his forties shouldn't play tennis. I heeded his advice carefully and could hardly wait until I reached fifty to start again.

Justice Hugo Black

When a man blames others for his failures, it's a good idea to credit others with his successes.

Howard W. Newton

If newspapers are useful in overthrowing tyrants, it is only to establish a tyranny of their own.

James Fenimore Cooper

One machine can do the work of fifty ordinary men. No machine can do the work of one extraordinary man.

Elbert Hubbard

Italians come to ruin most generally in three ways ... women, gambling, and farming. My family chose the slowest one.

Pope John XXIII

A bachelor is a man who never Mrs. anything.

I've met a few people in my time who were enthusiastic about hard work. It was just my luck that all of them happened to be men I was working for at the time.

Bill Gold

The only things that evolve by themselves in an organization are disorder, friction, and malperformance.

Peter Drucker

A bore is a person who deprives you of solitude without providing you with company.

Gian Vincenzo Lavina

Generally the theories we believe we call facts, and the facts we disbelieve we call theories.

Felix Cohen

I'm sixty-five and I guess that puts me in with the geriatrics, but if there were fifteen months in every year, I'd only be forty-eight.

James Thurber

There is a great deal of difference between an eager man who wants to read a book and the tired man who wants a book to read.

G. K. Chesterton

A child, like your stomach, doesn't need all you can afford to give it.

Unknown

We're all born brave, trusting and greedy, and most of us remain greedy.

Mignon McLaughlin

I am one individual on a small planet in a little solar system in one of the galaxies.

Roberto Assagioli

> *A true gentleman is one who invites you for a drink, opens the bottle and throws away the cork.*
>
> *George A. Brown*

Be Yourself ... is the worst advice you can give to some people.

Tom Masson

If an animal does something, we call it instinct; if we do the same thing for the same reason, we call it intelligence.

Will Cuppy

There is nobody so irritating as somebody with less intelligence and more sense than we have.

Don Herold

Compromise makes a good umbrella but a poor roof; it is a temporary expedient.

James Russel Lowell

High heels were invented by a woman who had been kissed on the forehead.

Christopher Morley

A great man is made up of qualities that meet or make great occasions.

James Russell Lowell

A miser is a guy who lives within his income. He's also called a magician.

Alliston Herald

Men make history and not the other way round. In periods where there is no leadership, society stands still. Progress occurs when courageous, skillful leaders seize the opportunity to change things for the better.

Harry S. Truman

It should be the function of medicine to have people die young as late as possible.

Ernst L. Wynder, M.D.

We can't all be heroes because someone has to sit on the curb and clap as they go by.

Will Rogers

Our middle classes who are comfortable and irresponsible at other people's expense, are neither ashamed of that condition nor even conscious of it.

George Bernard Shaw

The military and not the civilian authorities should be in charge of nuclear weapons.

General Edwin A. Walker

Millions say the apple fell ... but Newton was the one to ask why.

Bernard M. Baruch

I have offended God and mankind because my work didn't reach the quality it should have.

Leonardo da Vinci

When a man retires and time is no longer a matter of urgent importance, his colleagues generally present him with a watch.

R. C. Sherriff

True patriotism doesn't exclude an understanding of the patriotism of others.

Queen Elizabeth II

He who travels lightest travels furthest.

George A. Brown

The will to disbelieve is the strongest deterrent to wider horizons.

Hans Holzer

It is not the employer who pays wages ... he only handles the money. It is the product that pays wages.

Henry Ford

One kind of motorist who never runs out of gas is a back-seat driver.

The finest inheritance you can give to children is to allow them to make their own way, completely on their own feet.

Unknown

The indispensable requirement for a good newspaper ... as eager to tell a lie as the truth.

Norman Mailer

Whenever two people meet there are really six people present. There is each man as he sees himself, each man as the other person sees him, and each man as he really is.

William James

Law, in a democracy, means the protection of the rights and liberties of the minority.

Alfred E. Smith

The safest way to double your money is to fold it over once and put it in your pocket.

Frank McKinney Hubbard

It is always the best policy to speak the truth, unless, of course, you are an exceptionally good liar.

Jerome K. Jerome

Too often a sense of loyalty depends on admiration, and if we can't admire it is difficult to be loyal.

Aimee Buchanan

To love is to admire with the heart; to admire is to love with the mind.

Theophile Gautier

The hardest thing to learn in life is which bridge to cross and which to burn.

David Russell

I got the bill for my surgery. Now I know why those doctors were wearing masks.

James H. Boren

Diplomacy has rarely been able to gain at the conference table what cannot be gained or held on the battlefield.

General Walter Bedell Smith

Liberty is being free from the things we don't like in order to be slaves of the things we do like.

Ernest Benn

Never learn to do anything: if you don't learn, you'll always find someone else to do it for you.

Mark Twain

To live in minds we leave behind, is to be eternal.

Margo D. Brown

A real patriot is the fellow who gets a parking ticket and rejoices that the system works.

Bill Vaughan

The great thing in this world is not so much where we are, but in what direction we are going.

Oliver Wendell Holmes

The weak can never forgive. Forgiveness is the attribute of the strong...hatred can be overcome only by love.

Mahatma Gandhi

Inventing is a combination of brains and materials. The more brains you use, the less material you need.

Charles F. Kettering

Fear is letting go of something you treasure.

George A. Brown

When you see a light at the end of the tunnel, it means there's a train headed your way.

Tomorrow is the most important thing in life. Comes into us at midnight very clean. It's perfect when it arrives and it puts itself in our hands. It hopes we've learned something from yesterday.

John Wayne

Treasure the love you receive above all. It will survive long after your gold and good health have vanished.

Og Mandino

Never lend books, for no one ever returns them; the only books I have in my library are books that other folk have lent me.

Anatole France

I find that a great part of the information that I have was acquired by looking up something and finding something else on the way.

Franklin P. Adams

Wisdom only comes with experience. In the meantime, a good sense of humour certainly helps.

George A. Brown

PROVERBS

A bad excuse is better than none.

A bird in hand is worth two in the bush.

A broken friendship may be soldered.

A bull in a china shop.

A cat has nine lives.

A chip off the old block.

A cock-and-bull story.

A cold hand and a warm heart.

A constant guest is never welcome.

A drowning man will catch at a straw.

A drunken night makes a cloudy morning.

A fair exchange is no robbery.

A fool and his money are soon parted.

A fox is not taken twice in the same snare.

A friend in need is a friend indeed.

A friend to everybody is a friend to nobody.

A good archer is not known by his arrows, but his aim.

A good beginning makes a good ending.

A good conscience is a continual feast.

A good deed is never lost.

A good example is the best sermon.

A good face needs no paint.

A good life is the only religion.

A good surgeon must have an eagle's eye, a lion's heart, and a lady's hand.

A good tale is none the worse for being twice told.

A great fortune is a great slavery.

A guilty conscience needs no accuser.

A hair of the dog that bites you.

A hard nut to crack.

A heavy purse makes a light heart.

A hedge between keeps friendship.

A journey of a thousand miles must begin with a single step.

A liar is not believed when he speaks the truth.

A lie begets a lie.

A man is known by the company he keeps.

A man is as old as he feels, and a woman as old as she looks.

A man may lead a horse to the water but he cannot make him drink.

A miss is as good as a mile.

A new broom sweeps clean.

A penny for your thoughts.

A rolling stone gathers no moss.

A short life and a merry one.

A small leak will sink a great ship.

A stitch in time saves nine.

A tree is known by its fruit.

A woman's work is never done.

Absence makes the heart grow fonder.

Actions speak louder than words.

Adversity makes a man wise, not rich.

Advise none to marry or go to war.

Afraid of his own shadow.

After a storm comes a calm.

Agree, for the law is costly.

All good things come to an end.

All is fair in love and war.

All is not gold that glitters.

All is not lost that is in danger.

All is over bar (but) the shouting.

All is well that ends well.

All roads lead to Rome.

All tarred with the same brush.

All the world and his wife.

All things are difficult before they are easy.

All things come to those who wait.

All work and no play makes Jack a dull boy.

An apple a day keeps the doctor away.

An Englishman's home is his castle.

An honest man's word is an good as his bond.

An hour in the morning is worth two in the evening.

An hour of pain is as long as a day of pleasure.

An iron hand in a velvet glove.

An old head on young shoulders.

An old poacher makes a good game-keeper.

An ounce of discretion is worth a pound of learning.

Any port in a storm.

Art has no enemy except ignorance.

As a man lives, so shall he die.

As blind as a bat.

As clean as a whistle.

As dead as a doornail.

As drunk as a lord.

As dull as ditchwater.

As fit as a fiddle.

As flat as a pancake.

As hard as a rock.

As large as life.

As like as two peas.

As mad as a March hare.

As neat as a new pin.

As old as the hills.

As plain as the nose on a man's face.

As pleased as punch.

As poor as a church mouse.

As proud as a peacock.

As quiet as a mouse.

As right as rain.

As sick as a dog.

As slippery as an eel.

As soon as a man is born he begins to die.

As sure as an egg is an egg.

As thick as thieves.

As ugly as sin.

As warm as toast.

Ask no questions and you will be told no lies.

Back again, like a bad penny.

Barking dogs seldom bite.

Be a friend to thyself and others will befriend thee.

Beauty is but skin-deep.

Beauty is in the eye of the beholder.

Before one can say Jack Robinson.

Beggars cannot be choosers.

Better a lean peace than a fat victory.

Better an open enemy than a false friend.

Better be alone than in bad company.

Better be born lucky than rich.

Better be envied than pitied.

Better be happy than wise.

Better buy than borrow.

Better late than never.

Better luck next time.

Better never begin than never make an end.

Better some of a pudding than none of a pie.

Better suffer ill than do ill.

Better the devil you know than the devil you don't know.

Better the last smile than the first laughter.

Better to be safe than sorry.

Better untaught than ill-taught.

Between the devil and the deep blue sea.

Between you and me and the gate post.

Birds of a feather flock together.

Blessings are not valued till they are gone.

Blood is thicker than water.

Books and friends should be few and good.

Boys will be boys.

Bread is the staff of life.

Business before pleasure.

Butter would not melt in his mouth.

By hook or by crook.

By the skin of one's teeth.

Charity begins at home.

Children should be seen and not heard.

Choose a wife rather by your ear than your eye.

Choose neither a woman nor linen by candle-light.

Christmas comes but once a year..But when it comes it brings good cheer.

Civility costs nothing.

Cleanliness is next to godliness.

Confession is good for the soul.

Constant dropping wears away the stone.

Creditors have better memories than debtors.

Crocodile tears.

Crooked by nature is never made straight by education.

Curiosity killed the cat.

Custom is second nature.

Dead men tell no tales.

Death defies the doctor.

Debt is the worst poverty.

Desperate diseases must have desperate remedies.

Discretion is the better part of valour.

Divide and rule - *Divide et impera*.

Do as I say, not as I do.

Do not put all your eggs in one basket.

Dogs that bark at a distance never bite.

Don't count your chickens before they've hatched.

Don't cross the bridge till you get to it.

Drawn wells are seldom dry.

Drunken folks seldom take harm.

Early to bed and early to rise, makes a man healthy, wealthy and wise.

Easier said than done.

East or west, home is best.

Easy come, easy go.

Eat to live, but do not live to eat.

Education begins a gentleman, conversation completes him.

Either feast of famine.

Enough is as good as a feast.

Enough is enough.

Every cloud has a silver lining.

Every couple is not a pair.

Every dog has his day.

Every door may be shut but death's door.

Every little helps.

Every man for himself, and God for us all.

Every man has his faults.

Every man is best known to himself.

Everybody's business is nobody's business.

Everything comes to him who waits.

Everything is the worse for wearing.

Everything must have a beginning.

Experience is good, if not bought too dear.

Experience teaches - *Experientia docet*.

Faint heart never won fair lady.

Familiarity breeds contempt.

Far from eye, far from heart.

Faults are thick where love is thin.

Feed a cold and starve a fever.

Few words are best.

Finding's keeping.

Fire is a good servant but a bad master.

First come, first served.

First impressions are most lasting.

First think, and then speak.

Fling dirt enough, and some will stick.

Follow the river and you'll get to the sea.

Forewarned, forearmed.

Forgive and forget.

Friendship should not be all on one side.

From pillar to post.

Full of courtesy, full of craft.

Give a lie twenty-four hours' start, and you can never overtake it.

Give a thief rope enough and he'll hang himself.

Give him an inch and he'll take an mile.

Give the devil his due.

God defend me from my friends; from my enemies I can defend myself.

God heals, and the doctor takes the fee.

God helps them that help themselves.

God send me a friend that will tell me of my faults.

God tempers the wind to the shorn lamb.

God's mill grinds slow but sure.

Grasp all, lose all.

Great minds think alike.

Great souls have wills; feeble ones have only wishes.

Half a loaf is better than no bread.

Half the world knows not how the other half lives.

Hand and glove.

Handsome is that handsome does.

Happiness takes no account of time.

Happy is he that is happy in his children.

Happy is the country which has no history.

Haste makes waste.

Hatred is blind, as well as love.

Have but few friends though many acquaintances.

He deserves not the sweet that will not taste the sour.

He does not believe that does not live according to his belief.

He hath a good judgement that relieth not wholly on his own.

He is a fool who makes his doctor his heir.

He is a good friend that speaks well of us behind our backs.

He is lifeless that is faultless.

He is not a wise man who cannot play the fool on occasion.

He is rich that is satisfied.

He is worth his weight in gold.

He laughs best who laughs last.

He loses his thanks who promises and delays.

He should have a long spoon that sups with the devil.

He that comes first to the hill may sit where he will.

He that does you an ill turn will never forgive you.

He that fears death lives not.

He that fears you present will hate you absent.

He that fights and runs away may live to fight another day.

He that hath no head, needs no hat.

He that is too secure is not safe.

He that knows little, soon repeats it.

He that lies upon the ground can fall no lower.

He that respects not is not respected.

He that seeks trouble, never misses.

He that spares the bad injures the good.

He that speaks ill of his wife, dishonours himself.

He that thinks too much of his virtues bids others think of his vices.

He that travels far, knows much.

He that will not be counselled cannot be helped.

He that would commence many things finished but few.

He that would the daughter win, must with the mother first begin.

He was born with a silver spoon in his mouth.

He who knows nothing doubts nothing.

He who pays the piper may call the tune.

Heads I win, tails you lose.

Health is better than wealth.

Health is not valued till sickness come.

Hear the other side - *Audi alteram partem.*

Hear twice before you speak once.

Hearts may agree though heads differ.

Here to-day and gone to-morrow.

His bark is worse than his bite.

His heart is in his mouth.

His money burns a hole in his pocket.

History repeats itself.

Honesty is the best policy.

Honey in the mouth saves the purse.

Hope for the best and prepare for the worst.

Hot love is soon cold.

I was not born yesterday.

I will trust him no further than I can fling him.

If a job's worth doing, it's worth doing well.

If a man deceives me once, shame on him; if he deceives me twice, shame on me.

If the shoe fits, wear it.

If you bow at all, bow low.

If you can't be good be careful.

If you don't like it, you can lump it.

If you want a thing well done, do it yourself.

If your ears burn, someone is talking about you.

Ill doers are ill thinkers.

Ill gotten, ill spent.

In at one ear and out at the other.

In doing we learn.

In for a penny, in for a pound.

In the land of the blind, the one-eyed man is king.

It costs more to do ill than to do well.

It is a poor heart that never rejoices.

It is all in the day's work.

It is an ill wind that blows nobody good.

It is an equal failing to trust everybody, and to trust nobody.

It is better to weep with wisemen than to laugh with fools.

It is easier to pull down than to build.

It is easier to ridicule than commend.

It is easy to be wise after the event.

It is Greek to me.

It is hard to teach an old dog tricks.

It is hard to please all.

It is ill striving against the stream.

It is love that makes the world go around.

It is never a bad day that hath a good night.

It is never too late to mend.

It is no use crying over spilt milk.

It is not how long, but how well we live.

It is riches of the mind only that make a man rich and happy.

It is the men who make a city.

It is the blood of a soldier that makes a great general.

It is the unforeseen (unexpected) that always happens.

It is the nature of the beast.

It never rains but it pours.

It signifies nothing to play well if you lose.

It takes all sorts to make a world

It takes two to make a quarrel.

Jack of all trades and master of none.

Keep your mouth shut and your eyes open.

Kill not the goose that lays the golden eggs.

Kiss and be friends.

Know thyself.

Knowledge is no burden.

Knowledge is power.

Last but not least.

Law makers should not be law breakers.

Learn wisdom by the follies of others.

Least said, soonest mended.

Least talk most work.

Lend your money and lose your friend.

Let bygones be bygones.

Let sleeping dogs lie.

Let the buyer beware - *Caveat emptor.*

Let well alone.

Liars should have good memories.

Life is half spent before we know what it is.

Life is sweet.

Like a fish out of water.

Like a house on fire.

Like father, like son.

Like mother, like daughter.

Like water off a duck's back.

Little and often fills the purse.

Live and learn.

Live and let live.

Lock, stock, and barrel.

Long absent, soon forgotten.

Look before you leap.

Look on the bright side.

Losers seekers, finders keepers.

Love begets love.

Love is blind.

Love makes the world go round.

Love me little, love me long.

Love will find a way.

Mad as a hatter.

Make hay while the sun shines.

Make the best of a bad bargain.

Man in the moon.

Man or mouse.

Many a true word is spoken in jest.

Many hands make light work.

March comes in like a lion and goes out like a lamb.

Marry in haste and repent at leisure.

Measure thrice before you cut once.

Men are blind in their own cause.

Mind your own business.

Misfortunes never come singly.

Money begets money.

Money is a good servant, but a bad master.

Money talks.

Much law, but little justice.

Natural folly is bad enough, but learned folly is intolerable.

Necessity hath no law.

Necessity is the mother of invention.

Never ask pardon before you are accused.

Never cross a bridge till you come to it.

Never do things by halves.

Never judge a book by its cover.

Never look a gift horse in the mouth.

Never put off till to-morrow what may be done to-day.

Never refuse a good offer.

Never say die.

Never too old to learn.

Never trouble trouble till trouble troubles you.

No fool like an old fool.

No gains without pains.

No news is good news.

No pleasure without pain.

No rose without a thorn.

No smoke without some fire.

No sunshine but has some shadow.

No taxation without representation.

No time like the present.

No wisdom like silence.

None knows the weight of another's burden.

None so blind as those who won't see.

None so deaf as those who won't hear.

Not room to swing a cat.

Not to be fit to hold a candle to him.

Not to be sneezed at.

Nothing costs so much as what is given us.

Nothing is certain but uncertainty.

Nothing is certain but death and taxes.

Nothing is impossible to a willing heart.

Nothing is ours, but time.

Nothing seek, nothing find.

Nothing so bad but it might have been worse.

Nothing succeeds like success.

Nothing ventured, nothing gained.

Of two evils, choose the least.

Old friends and old wine are best.

On the spur of the moment.

Once bitten, twice shy.

One beats the bush, and another catches the birds.

One cannot be in two places at once.

One enemy is too many, and a hundred friends too few.

One good turn deserves another.

One hour's sleep before midnight is worth three after.

One law for the rich and another for the poor.

One man's meat is another man's poison.

One must draw the line somewhere.

One must draw back in order to leap better - *Il faut reculer pour mieux sauter.*

One swallow does not make a summer.

One to-day is worth two tomorrows.

Out of sight, out of mind.

Out of the frying-pan into the fire.

Patience is a flower that grows not in everyone's garden.

Patience, money and time bring all things to pass.

Penny wise, pound foolish.

Pension never enriched a young man.

People who live in glass houses should never throw stones.

Possession is nine points of the law.

Poverty breeds strife.

Poverty is not a shame, but the being ashamed of it is.

Practice makes perfect.

Practice what you preach.

Praise makes good men better and bad men worse.

Prevention is better than cure.

Pride will have a fall.

Put that in your pipe and smoke it.

Put your shoulder to the wheel.

Rain before seven: fine before eleven.

Rain, rain, go to Spain: fair weather come again.

Rats desert a sinking ship.

Religion is the best armour in the world, but the worst cloak.

Revenge never repairs an injury.

Rome was not built in a day.

Rule youth well, for age will rule itself.

Save it for a rainy day.

Save your breath to cool your porridge.

Saying is one thing and doing another.

Second thoughts are best.

Seeing is believing.

Self-praise is no recommendation.

Self-preservation is the first law of nature.

Set a thief to catch a thief.

Share and share alike.

Short and sweet.

Short pleasure, long lament.

Silence gives consent.

Six of one and half a dozen of the other.

Slow but sure.

Small things amuse little minds.

So far, so good.

Some are wise and some are otherwise.

Soon got, soon spent.

Soon ripe, soon rotten.

Sour grapes can never make sweet wine.

Spare the rod and spoil the child.

Speak well of your friend, of your enemy say nothing.

Speak when you are spoken to.

Speech is silver, silence is golden.

Spick and span.

Sticks and stones may break my bones, but words will never hurt me.

Stiff as a poker.

Still waters run deep.

Strike while the iron is hot.

Subtlety is better than force.

Take away my good name and take away my life.

Take care of the pence and the pounds will take care of themselves.

Take things as you find them.

Tell that to the Marines.

That is a game that two can play at.

That is but an empty purse that is full of other men's money.

That is well spoken that is well taken.

That which was bitter to endure may be sweet to remember.

The absent are always in the wrong.

The best mirror is an old friend.

The boot is on the other leg.

The busiest men have the most leisure.

The coast is clear.

The company makes the feast.

The darkest hour is before the dawn.

The day has eyes and the night has ears.

The early bird catches the worm.

The end justifies the means.

The English never know when they are beaten.

The evening crowns the day.

The exception proves the rule.

The fat is in the fire.

The first blow is half the battle.

The first faults are theirs that commit them, the second theirs that permit them.
The fool wanders, the wise man travels.
The fox knows much, but more he that catcheth him.
The greatest hate springs from the greatest love.
The greatest talkers are always the least doers.
The higher up, the greater the fall.
The last straw breaks the camel's back.
The longest day must have an end.
The man in the street.
The more haste, the less speed.
The more laws, the more offenders.
The more the merrier, the fewer the better cheer.
The mother-in-law remembers not that she was a daughter-in-law.
The noblest vengeance is to forgive.
The pleasure of what we enjoy is lost by coveting more.
The pot calls the kettle black.
The proof of the pudding is in the eating.
The road to hell is paved with good intentions.
The shortest answer is doing.
The sight of you is good for sore eyes.
The stone that lieth not in your way need not offend you.
The sun shines upon all alike.
The tongue is ever turning to the aching tooth.
The tongue is not steel, yet it cuts.
The tongue of idle people is never idle.
The truth, the whole truth, and nothing but the truth.
The way to a man's heart is through his stomach.
The way to be safe is never to be secure.
The weakest goes to the wall.
The wish is father to the thought.
The worth of a thing is best known by the want.
There are two sides to every story.
There is a remedy for all things but death.
There is a snake in the grass.
There is a time for all things.
There is a measure in all things.
There is a screw loose somewhere.
There is honour among thieves.
There is more pleasure in loving than in being loved.
There is no love lost between them.
There is no accounting for tastes.
There is only one pretty child in the world, and every mother has it.
There would be no great ones if there were no little ones.
There's many a slip 'twixt the cup and the lip.
They love too much that die for love.
Think today and speak tomorrow.
Think well of all men.
Thinking is very far from knowing.

Time and thinking tame the strongest grief.
Time and tide wait for no man.
Time flies - *Tempus fugit.*
To add insult to injury.
To bark up the wrong tree.
To be all in the same boat.
To be at sixes and sevens.
To be in a person's good (or bad) books.
To be on one's last legs.
To be too big for one's boots.
To beat about the bush.
To blow one's own trumpet.
To build castles in the air.
To build castles in Spain.
To burn the candle at both ends.
To burn the midnight oil.
To bury the hatchet.
To buy and sell, and live by the loss.
To call a spade a spade.
To come up to scratch.
To cook one's own goose.
To cool one's heels.
To cry "Wolf".
To cut off one's nose to spite one's face.
To eat one's words.
To err is human - *Humanum est errare.*
To fiddle while Rome is burning.
To flog a dead horse.
To get blood out of a stone.
To give the cold shoulder.
To go scot-free.
To haul over the coals.
To have a sweet tooth.
To have a bee in one's bonnet.
To have a finger in the pie.
To have an axe to grind.
To have bats in the belfry.
To have many irons in the fire.
To have one foot in the grave.
To hit the nail on the head.
To keep a stiff upper lip.
To keep one's nose to the grindstone.
To keep the wolf from the door.
To keep up with the Joneses.
To kill two birds with one stone.
To know on which side one's bread is buttered.
To know the ropes.
To know where the shoe pinches.
To know which way the wind blows.
To leave in the lurch.
To leave no stone unturned.
To let the cat out of the bag.
To line one's pockets.
To look for a needle in a haystack.
To make a clean breast.
To make a mountain out of a molehill.

To make a person turn in his grave.
To make ends meet.
To make the best of a bad job.
To make two bites of a cherry.
To mind one's P's and Q's.
To pay a person in his own coin.
To pay through the nose.
To play second fiddle.
To pour oil upon the waters.
To pull the wool over a person's eyes.
To put on one's thinking cap.
To put one's best foot forward.
To put the cart before the horse.
To roar like a bull.
To rob Peter to pay Paul.
To rule the roost.
To run with the hare and hunt with the hounds.
To save one's bacon.
To smell a rat.
To sow one's wild oats.
To split hairs.
To stew in one's own juice.
To stir up a hornets' nest.
To take a leaf out of one's book.
To take one down a peg or two.
To take the bull by the horns.
To take the wind out of one's sails.
To take the law into one's own hands.
To talk the hind leg off a donkey.
To talk without thinking is to shoot without aiming.
To tell tales out of school.
To throw good money after bad.
To turn an honest penny.
To turn over a new leaf.
To turn the tables.
To turn up trumps.
To turn up one's nose.
To twist round one's little finger.
To upset the Apple-cart.
To warm the cockles of the heart.
To wear one's heart on one's sleeve.
To wet one's whistle.
Tomorrow is a new day.
Tomorrow never comes.
Too many cooks spoil the broth.
Touch wood.
Trust in god, but tie your camel.
Trust not a new friend nor an old enemy.
Truth is stranger than fiction.
Truth never grows old.

Two can play at that game.
Two heads are better than one.
Two is company, three is a crowd.
Two negatives make an affirmative.
Two wrongs don't make a right.
Unity is strength.
Variety is the spice of life.
Virtue never grows old.
Vows made in storms are forgotten in calm.
Wait and see.
Walls have ears.
Wars bring scars.
Waste not, want not.
We never miss the water till the well runs dry.
What can't be cured must be endured.
What is done by night appears by day.
What is sauce for the goose is sauce for the gander.
What is worth doing is worth doing well.
What soberness conceals, drunkenness reveals.
What the eye sees not, the heart rues not.
What you don't know can't hurt you.
What's yours is mine, and what's mine is my own.
Whatever will be, will be - *Che sera, sera.*
When I lend I am a friend, when I ask I am a foe.
When in doubt, leave out.
When one door shuts another opens.
When the cat is away the mice will play.
When we are pleased ourselves, we begin to please others.
Where there's a will, there's a way.
While there is life, there is hope.
Whom we love best, to them we can say least.
Wine in, truth out.
Wise men learn by other men's mistakes; fools by their own.
Wonders will never cease.
You can't take it with you when you go.
You cannot eat your cake and have it.
You cannot lose what you never had.
You cannot make a silk purse out of a sow's ear.
You cannot see the forest for the trees.
You might have heard a pin drop.
You might have knocked me down with a feather.
You scratch my back and I'll scratch yours.
Young men think old men fools, and old men know young men to be so.
Zeal is fit only for wise men, but is found mostly in fools.
Zeal without knowledge is fire without light.

ABOUT THE AUTHOR

George A. Brown is a well-known military historian and he has previously published nine books and numerous articles on military history. He is a well-known expert on military medals both in Canadian and International circles. He was born in Belleville, Ontario and raised in Toronto, Ontario. He has lived most of his life in the Vancouver area of British Columbia. He is a member of the Insurance Brokers Association of British Columbia and an Associate of the Insurance Institute of Canada (AIIC). He is a past president of the Military Collector's Club of Canada. A member of the Orders and Medals Society of Great Britain, Orders and Medals Society of America, Canadian Heraldry Society, the United Empire Loyalists and founder of the Canadian Guild of Authors. George is a recipient of a number of decorations of several countries including the Freedom of the City of London, England. He has developed a keen interest in books which led him to researching and ultimately the writing of many books and articles on military history. This book entitled The Book of Wisdom and Wit is his first breakthrough from his traditional writing.

It is anticipated that a sequel to The Book of Wisdom and Wit will be produced in the near future. It is planned that this next book will be entitled The Book of Wit and Wisdom, therefore, if you have any remarks that you would like to share with other readers please forward them to:

George A. Brown

P. O. Box 3095

Langley, B. C.

V3A 4R3

A credit will be given to all those contributors.

The Book of Wisdom and Wit makes a great and original gift. Call toll-free in Canada 1-800-663-9066 and/or your nearest bookstore for current price information.